BRITISH
STUFF

BRITISH STUFF

Summersdale Publishers Ltd
46 West Street
Chichester
West Sussex
PO19 1RP
UK

www.summersdale.com

Printed and bound in China

ISBN: 978-1-84953-368-3

Disclaimer
Every effort has been made to ensure that credits accurately comply with the information
supplied. Should there be any omissions or errors in this respect we apologise and will be
pleased to make the appropriate acknowledgements in any future editions.

Substantial discounts on bulk quantities of Summersdale books are available to corporations,
professional associations and other organisations. For details contact Nicky Douglas by telephone
(+44-1243-756902), fax (+44-1243-786300) or email (nicky@summersdale.com).

BRITISH STUFF

Life in Britain through
101 everyday objects

Geoff Hall
Kamila Kasperowicz

Contents:

Introduction

When we arrive in a foreign country it is the objects in everyday use that strike us first, often within minutes of our arrival. The cars, food, clothes and signs that we take for granted at home are all different here. How is it different countries come up with such varied solutions for the same basic needs?

This book was inspired by a love of physical objects: things that you can see, touch, smell and in some cases taste. Not old objects, but the ones with which we are most familiar. Objects appeal to our senses, but they often have stories to tell as well: stories about how they came into being, about why they have survived and how their significance has changed over time.

In a globalised world where new ideas are communicated instantly, more and more of the objects we use are international in nature. It is often difficult to attribute an individual object to any one nation.

The iPhone, for example, was designed by a British designer, Jonathan Ives, it is assembled in China and marketed by an American company, Apple. Not just that, but you are as likely to find it in the hands of an office worker in Shanghai or an IT professional in Mumbai, as in those of a lawyer in New York or a banker in London.

For over 200 years Britain has been an international power and many of the ideas and products which originated there, especially sports like cricket and tennis, have been exported around the world. Britain has in turn imported many things from other countries – from tea to wallpaper – and adapted them to meet its own needs.

All this may lead us to conclude that there could not possibly be very much left that is distinctively British. And yet, when visitors come to Britain and Britons visit other countries, they immediately recognise differences. It is not just about the buildings or the language. It is about the clothes, hats and shoes that people wear, the food they eat, the transport they use and the objects they employ in their daily lives.

Alongside this there is a growing interest in what has come to be known as 'material culture', an awareness that this 'stuff' should not simply be dismissed as mere examples of a shallow 'materialist' world, but recognised as objects that tell valuable and interesting stories about 21st century people and their lives.

The objects that have been included in this book have been chosen using four main criteria:

Firstly, the objects selected all have some distinctively British flavour or characteristic. They are things that would strike, say, a Chinese visitor to Britain as unusual or different from what they would find at home.

Secondly, we have included only objects that have some element of man-made design, so you will not find primroses or oak trees here, even though some might consider them quintessentially British.

Thirdly, the objects are all in current use, not folk objects from a museum. It is true that some may only be used by a minority, often older people, or be more heavily used in one part of the country than another, but they will still be in regular use and recognised as such. Some may be luxury products, like the Rolls–Royce Phantom, available only to a privileged few, but most will not.

Finally, the objects help build a broader picture of life in Britain today. Not a complete one of course, because Britain is one of the most multicultural countries in the world and many first and second generation immigrants who are now British citizens will have their own sets of distinctive 'stuff'.

We have excluded buildings and landmarks too. So no Buckingham Palace or Ann Hathaway's cottage, no Paddington Station or Houses of Parliament.

What we want to capture are the things that people can see anywhere in Britain, that British people use every day, and that above all contribute in some way to their own sense of identity.

Mini

The Mini is one of those rare products that has evolved over time from functional workhorse to fashion icon. It was designed in the late 1950s by the British Motor Corporation as a pratical, fuel-efficient family car. At that time three-wheel bubble cars were the only choice for motorists who needed a small, economical car. The Mini was revolutionary because its transverse engine, front-wheel drive layout left plenty of space for four passengers, with luggage, in a car just 3 m long.

To begin with, sales were slow as the Mini gained a reputation for being unreliable and complicated to fix. But then, in the early 1960s, two things happened. First the Mini Cooper proved to be a great (and unexpected) success in motor racing and rallying. Then a number of celebrities, including the actor Peter Sellers and the Beatles, were seen in Minis.

Soon the Mini became associated with the swinging London fashion and music scene of the 1960s, and its starring role in the hit film *The Italian Job* in 1969 cemented its success. Even as late as 2002 the Mini continued to enjoy a starring role, this time in the car chase in *The Bourne Identity*, with Matt Damon at the wheel of an elderly mini, successfully evading the Paris police.

In the 1960s students competed with one another to see who could get the most people into a Mini. This continued long after the original Mini went out of production in 2000, the current record being set in 2006 by a group of Spaniards, who proved that you can fit 22 people (but probably not in great comfort) into a Mini.

The Mini stayed in production for more than 40 years. Almost 5.5 million cars had been produced in that

time, and an internet poll conducted by the Global Automotive Elections Foundation in 1999 voted the Mini European Car of the Century. For the top prize of World Car of the Century it was beaten only by the pioneering Ford Model T.

More importantly the Mini had established itself as a style icon, and many of its distinctive design features have been carried on in the new MINI – now owned by the German company BMW, but still built in Britain – which was launched in 2001 and is now exported all over the world.

Owners of the new MINI seem to form the same kind of bond with their cars that drivers of the old one did. Every year owners of both old and new Minis are invited to take part in 'The Italian Job, a driving adventure' from Italy to the UK, which harks back to

the 1969 film. Run since 1990, 'The Italian Job' claims to have raised over £2 million for children's charities – and by all reports, provided a lot of fun for its participants along the way. ■

You can fit 22 people (but probably not in great comfort) into a Mini

Lea & Perrins Worcestershire Sauce

Whilst many companies sell a product under the title of Worcester (pronounced woos-tah) Sauce, the original – The Original & Genuine Lea & Perrins Worcestershire Sauce, to give it its full name – is the one illustrated here. Still made at the Midland Road factory in Worcester set up to produce it in 1897, Lea & Perrins is often added to savoury dishes like casseroles, chilli con carne and Welsh rarebit. One cookbook even proposes its use in a summer strawberry salad. It is probably best known, however, for its starring role alongside vodka and tomato juice in the Bloody Mary cocktail.

Messrs Lea and Perrins were pharmacists who owned a shop in Worcester. The story goes that in 1835 a local nobleman returning from Bengal gave them a recipe that he had brought back from India. The two chemists set about recreating the sauce, after acquiring the necessary and, for them, quite exotic ingredients. They followed the recipe but the results were disappointing. All agreed that the sauce tasted terrible. Instead of pouring it away they bottled it and left it in their cellars. When they rediscovered the jars some time later they tasted it once again and discovered that it had fermented into a delicious savoury sauce.

The reputation of the sauce quickly spread and Messrs Lea and Perrins decided to manufacture it. In 1837 they started to sell the product under the now familiar Lea & Perrins name. Within six years their energetic marketing campaigns had increased sales dramatically to some 14,500 bottles a year – a significant amount for a product which (like English mustard) is only used sparingly. In 1849 they started to export it to New York.

Although Lea & Perrins were keen to protect their secret recipe, other manufacturers naturally wanted to share in its success and started making their own versions of the sauce. In 1906 Lea & Perrins took one rival to court, claiming that they had the exclusive right to make Worcestershire sauce. The court found against Lea & Perrins, but did permit them the exclusive right to call theirs 'original and genuine', a phrase which still appears prominently on the label today.

Given the care the company took to protect the secrecy of its recipe, many were surprised when Brian Keogh, an accountant at Lea & Perrins in the 1970s, revealed that he had found notes dating back to the 1880s in a skip outside the factory, which listed the ingredients (he never explained exactly why he was rooting around in the skip in the first place). The notes did not, however, show the full details required to reproduce the sauce. The list included vinegar, molasses, sugar, salt, anchovies, tamarind extract, onions, garlic, spice, and flavouring – the latter believed to include cloves, soy sauce, lemons, pickles and peppers.

Mix all those together and leave for 18 months and you have Worcestershire sauce. Or not. Or you could just buy a bottle. ■

All agreed that the sauce tasted terrible

Postage stamp

Until the early 19th century there was no simple way to send a letter in Britain, or anywhere else for that matter. Postal services were chaotic and unreliable. Postage was not paid by the sender but by the recipient of the letter and this presented two main problems. Firstly, if the recipient refused to pay then there was no way to recover the cost of delivering the letter. And secondly, if the sender did not have to pay he or she had no incentive to minimise the size and weight of the letter. In addition postal charges could be very complicated as they had to take account of letter size, weight and distance travelled.

In 1837 Victoria became Queen of England, a role that she was to fulfil for the next 64 years, through the heyday of the British Empire. Around the same time an Englishman, Sir Rowland Hill produced a document entitled 'Post Office Reform: Its Importance and Practicability', which he presented to the government, paving the way for the postal system which now operates in most countries around the world.

Rowland Hill's idea – and one which was strongly resisted by the Post Office at that time – was to charge the same fee regardless of distance travelled, with postage paid by the sender. At the same time he introduced the idea of the postage stamp. Until that time postage had been recorded by banging an inked stamp on to the letter, now instead it was

to be done by using a pre-gummed piece of paper showing the standard charge for all letters, one penny.

The first adhesive stamp, known as the Penny Black, was introduced in May 1840 and bore Queen Victoria's head on it. Many people assume that Penny Blacks must be very valuable, but in fact they are not exceptionally rare. The early penny post service was so popular that over the first ten years of its life over 68 million Penny Blacks were issued and many survive, though a mint stamp can, it is true, fetch several thousand pounds. In 1841 the Penny Black was replaced by the Penny Red, the change of colour making it easier to see when a stamp had been cancelled. The Penny Red became the first perforated stamp – until then the stamps had to be cut from a printed sheet using scissors.

Every British stamp since the first Penny Black has borne the head of the reigning monarch, always in profile with each King or Queen facing the opposite way from his or her predecessor. As these were the very first stamps anywhere, no one thought to put the name of the country on British stamps. So, even though postage stamps are not a uniquely British phenomenon, to this day Britain remains the only country in the world not to carry the name of the country on its stamps. ∎

To this day Britain remains the only country in the world not to carry the name of the country on its stamps

Hille E Series chair

If you visit any school assembly hall, company restaurant or village hall in Britain you will likely encounter one of the many versions of the Hille stackable polypropylene chair. Designed by Robin Day in 1963, between 14 and 20 million have been produced since then. Cheap to produce, strong, lightweight, hard-wearing and easy to stack, the Hille chair is a rare example of a design icon so effective and ubiquitous that it has become almost invisible.

Robin Day graduated from the Royal College of Art in 1938, but his career as a designer was put on hold by World War Two. After the war he and his wife, Lucienne, became famous, she working in textile design and he in furniture. In 1948 Day submitted a design for wooden storage units to an international competition for low-cost furniture organised by The Museum of Modern Art in New York.

His innovative use of moulded plywood not only secured him first prize but also attracted the attention of furniture manufacturer Hille International, who wanted to extend their furniture range to include more contemporary designs. From 1949 Hille sponsored Day, and he went on to produce over 150 products, including office chairs, desks and storage, as well as public seating for major London venues like the Tate Gallery, Barbican Centre and London Underground.

Day's designs reflect the time in which he was working. Instead of the heavy and often cumbersome furniture designs which went before, Day's chairs are more delicate, with thin legs and they use the minimum of materials (an important factor in the austerity of post-war Britain).

Although the polypropylene chair now looks commonplace, it was radical for its time. The brief from Hille called for a low-cost stacking chair, which could be mass-produced and used in a wide range of situations. Polypropylene itself had only been invented (by an Italian, Giulio Natta) nine years earlier and few

'This chair is one of the ugliest pieces of design I have ever had to endure during years and years of torture in classrooms'

companies had expertise in injection moulding it. The chair's folded edges not only give it extra strength but also make it easier to pick up and slot into place when stacking. The lip on the sides allows each chair to sit directly on top of the one below, stopping the stack from leaning over as it gets higher.

Making the seat and back out of one single moulding greatly simplified assembly, helping to keep the cost of manufacture down. This closely reflected Day's design philosophy, one driven by function – ergonomics, efficient use of materials and ease of manufacture – rather than flashiness.

The original design, known as the Polyside chair, was replaced by the E Series in 1972.

It is true that not all users of the chair, especially those who associate it with unhappy schooldays, consider it such an ergonomic success. One online contributor to a design blog noted caustically, 'This chair is one of the ugliest pieces of design I have ever had to endure during years and years of torture in classrooms. It... made my back and arse sore, made it impossible to find a decent position, tortured the spine to acquire strange and damaging... shapes and must be the design equivalent of radioactivity.'

A more conventional assessment was offered by Bill Moggridge, Director of the National Design Museum in New York: 'I was halfway through my industrial design studies in London when Robin Day's stacking chair for Hille came out in 1963... I was immediately fascinated by the simplicity of the form combined with the deep understanding of the behaviour of the material.' ■

Anglepoise lamp

The Anglepoise lamp is an iconic design which has found its way around the world, but its origins and design retain uniquely British characteristics. Designed and developed not by a professional designer, but by an engineer, the Anglepoise was not the product of any coherent business-led R&D programme. Its 'designer' did not even set out to create a new lamp; instead the Anglepoise was the fruit of a technology in search of an application which could exploit it.

In 1932 an automotive engineer, George Carwardine, patented a new type of spring which could retain its position after being stretched or compressed. Carwardine owned a company in the west of England which specialised in vehicle suspension systems, but

it seems the research that led to the Anglepoise lamp was largely undertaken by him out of curiosity rather than to produce higher performance car springs. Aware of basic engineering principles and also the constant tension principle associated with the human arm, Carwardine spent two years developing what would become the Anglepoise. (Carwardine originally planned to call his light the Equipoise but was unable to register that name.)

His plan was that the lamp would be purely for industrial use. Because it could be adjusted to provide a highly focused light he thought it would be ideal for detailed assembly work.

In 1934 he licensed the light, but not to a lighting manufacturer. Instead the company of Herbert Terry & Sons, a manufacturer based at Redditch in Worcestershire which supplied springs, took up its development and marketing. Terry & Sons continue to supply variants of the original Anglepoise to this day, even though the patent was sold to the Norwegian lighting designer Jacob Jacobsen in 1937, and Jacobsen went on to create his own variant, the Luxor L-1, which achieved success in its own right.

The Anglepoise's mechanical appearance, with all its working parts on show, fitted neatly into the stripped down aesthetic of the age, even though it was probably never designed with any particular aesthetic in mind. Not only does it work exceptionally effectively, providing well directed light, but a big part of its appeal must lie in its resemblance to a human companion; the Anglepoise has a strangely benign appearance, like a hooded monk peeking encouragingly over your shoulder while you work. ∎

The Anglepoise has a strangely benign appearance, like a hooded monk peeking encouragingly over your shoulder while you work

Crumpet

A crumpet is a circular-shaped bread-like unsweetened cake made from flour and yeast. It usually has holes in in the top, which result from adding baking powder. Although it is easy to find recipes to make your own crumpets, generally people buy part-cooked crumpets at the supermarket and then toast them or heat them under a grill at home.

Most people would consider a crumpet an ideal snack with their afternoon tea, but what they choose to eat on their toasted crumpet is much more varied.

If you are really into crumpets then you will talk about eating yours 'dripping with butter', suggesting the last word in luxury, and you may then add further sweet or savoury toppings.

Sweet toppings might include honey, golden syrup or jam, whilst savoury accompaniments such as cheese, Marmite or a poached egg will be favoured by others.

If you grow up in a family that has always eaten crumpets with honey then it can be quite a shock

Not to be

confused with

a pikelet

when you leave home and discover that other people only eat them with Marmite or cheese.

There is also a regional variant of the crumpet called the pikelet. It is usually made from the same kind of batter as a crumpet, and in some parts of England, for example in the Birmingham area, a pikelet is simply a crumpet without holes. In other parts, such as around Manchester, a pikelet has holes, but is wider and thinner than a crumpet. In Wales a pikelet is very different from a crumpet and resembles what

in Scotland is called a pancake and in most parts of England is called a Scotch pancake. We hope that is all perfectly clear.

Before the rise of feminism – say, before the 1970s – it was not uncommon for men to refer to an attractive woman as 'crumpet' and for a woman who was both attractive and intelligent to be referred to as 'thinking man's crumpet', but if you use the word crumpet now to refer to a woman you will seem very out of date and rather sexist. ∎

K6 telephone kiosk

In 1924 the Post Office launched a competition to produce a new telephone kiosk. The winning design – called the K2 (Kiosk No. 2) – was created by Sir Giles Gilbert Scott, the architect who also created the Anglican Cathedral in Liverpool and London's Battersea Power Station.

The original wooden prototype K2 kiosk survives to this day and can be found in the entrance to the Royal Academy at Burlington House on Piccadilly in London, alongside a production version of the K2.

You can find what many believe to have been the designer's original inspiration for the phone box, in St Pancras Old Churchyard in London. It is the mausoleum which Sir John Soane designed for himself. The dome of the mausoleum strongly resembles that of the phone box, and Sir Giles Gilbert Scott just happened to be a trustee of Sir John Soane's Museum in Lincoln's Inn Fields at the time.

Scott originally intended his kiosk to be painted silver, with a blue-green interior. However, the Post Office decided to paint them red, so that they would be easier to see in an emergency. This was a controversial decision at the time, with many protests that the colour was garish and offensive. The Post Office did allow rural examples to be painted in different colours including green, yellow, white and grey.

In Hull (or Kingston upon Hull, to give it its full name) where the phone system was not run by the Post Office but by the local city council, they decided to paint their phone boxes cream and to remove the royal crown altogether.

The colour, however, was not their biggest problem. There was another, much larger one. The K2 was big and expensive to make, so in 1935 Scott came up with a revised version of the K2, which was smaller, lighter and cheaper to build – designated the K6.

The K6 kiosk appeared in 1936, followed by a more vandal-proof version in 1939. In the 1980s the Post Office was privatised and the new company, British Telecom tried to introduce alternative modernist designs in glass and steel featuring its new pale grey logo. The outcry against the loss of the popular red kiosk was as loud as that which had accompanied its introduction. (Ironically the objections were loudest in conservation areas, exactly the same areas that had protested against the introduction of the red phone box in the first place.) Because of the outcry, large numbers of the red kiosks have been preserved.

In 2012 locals in the fishing village of Killiemuir in Scotland set up a round-the-clock barricade of their local phone box to prevent BT engineers from removing it, arguing that it was needed for emergencies, such as in the case of a fishing accident. In their defence, BT pointed out that they had put up a notice inside the kiosk giving 90 days' notice of their intention to remove it, but it seems none of the villagers had spotted it.

This in itself points to the biggest problem facing the red phone box today. Over 90 per cent of adults in the United Kingdom now have a mobile phone, so, as much as people love the iconic red kiosks, few actually use them. In a survey carried out by BT only three per cent of the population said that they had actually used a BT Payphone recently, so it is perhaps not surprising that many of the old kiosks now look a little neglected.

But all is not lost. Recognising their popularity, BT launched its 'Adopt a Kiosk' scheme. Local communities can now take over their phone box, paying just £1 for it (after BT has removed the payphone equipment). Some communities have chosen to keep them simply for their appearance, planting flowers around them, but others have converted them into book exchanges (like the one pictured here at Sheepwash in Devon) or into miniature art galleries; one has even installed a defibrillator for emergency use.

The K6 has become not just a design icon but a real work of art. In Kingston upon Thames, artist David Mach toppled 12 kiosks against one another to create an artwork titled 'Out of Order', and graffiti artist Banksy had fun with another, cutting and rewelding it. You can see it in his film *Exit through the Giftshop*. ■

The K6 has become

not just a design icon

but a real work of art

Barbour jacket

The Barbour jacket is a Range Rover without the wheels... or an engine: it speaks of a rugged, outdoor life in the country even when it is cruising round the streets of Kensington or Chelsea. It may never get anywhere close to a fishing stream or a grouse moor in Scotland, but it makes you believe that it (and its wearer) could survive there just as easily if it had to. Wear it in Knightsbridge in the week; take it to the country at the weekend.

However, the Barbour's associations with a certain up-market, landed-gentry, London-based lifestyle could not be further from its origins. The company started out in the north east of England, in South Shields in 1894, and its waxed jackets are made there to this day. Its first customers were not the affluent middle and upper classes of the Home Counties. Instead they were the sailors and dockyard workers of Tyneside, who bought Barbour's waterproof oilskin jackets for strictly practical reasons – because they kept them warm and dry – and because they were durable. Over time it was natural for Barbour's market to extend to other activities that required people to be outdoors in all weathers: motorcyclists, horse riders, leisure fishermen and other country sports enthusiasts.

Even now a Barbour is designed to last a lifetime. In its collection Barbour has a jacket dating back to 1911, which belonged to three generations of the same family. To maximise its lifespan the company recommends you get your Barbour re-waxed once a year and it takes back thousands of jackets each year for just this purpose.

Recently, though, Barbour – which remains family-owned – has been making moves to shake off its traditional image and widen its appeal to a new, younger clientele. On its website you will find Barbour's Guide to Civilised Festival Attendance, a comic-style manual for those attending one of Britain's many summer music festivals. (Naturally, a good waterproof jacket is high on the list of recommended things you should take with you.) The firm has also engaged in collaborations with designers like Alice Temperley and with fashion companies like Paul Smith's R. Newbold brand to create a cooler urban streetwear collection.

Fashion may be the future for Barbour, but the joy of it is that it works. Function precedes fashion. Its shooting jacket features high pockets for easy access to shotgun cartridges; its motorcycle jacket will withstand wind-buffeting. Just as the Range Rover boasts the highest level of off-road capability (even if never required by most of its customers), so the Barbour is designed to see off the worst the British climate can throw at it.

On the one hand it boasts three royal warrants and supplies the royal estates with jackets, and on the other it clothes the likes of Kate Moss, Alexa Chung and the Arctic Monkeys, all of whom reputedly had to buy their Barbours... No freebie celebrity endorsements here. ■

Knightsbridge in the week.

Country at the weekend

Blackpool rock

Blackpool rock: a rod of hard, boiled sugar about 30 cm long and 2–3 cm in diameter, pink on the outside, white on the inside, with lettering running through its centre, flavoured with peppermint or spearmint.

It's never going to be confused with a health food and it's certainly not great for the teeth, but it is special for many people in Britain because a stick of rock is an instant reminder of an illicit treat during childhood holidays at the seaside – the kind of sweet bought by an indulgent grandparent when your parents were not looking. It is special too because it is one of those rare objects that makes you ask: how do they make that? How do they get the lettering to run all the way down a stick of rock?

Although some parts of the rock-making process can be handled by machine, much of it is still done by hand, especially the forming of the individual letters which are carefully rolled, stretched and twisted, one letter at a time, and then combined to form the finished word while the mixture is still warm. You can make any word, of course, and most large British

Never going to be confused with a health food

seaside towns will sell rock bearing their own name. Brighton rock became famous, for example, as the title of a Graham Greene novel and later as a film.

In the north of England it was Blackpool that became the supreme seaside resort. Over the course of the 19th century it grew from a small village into the prime holiday destination for the industrial working classes of Lancashire and Yorkshire. In 1801 the town had a population of 473; a century later it had grown a hundredfold – to over 47,000. What changed its fortunes was the arrival of the railway, which allowed industrial workers from Manchester and Leeds to reach it easily. Blackpool responded by creating cheap accommodation, entertainment and food. When the famous Blackpool tower was built in 1894 it was the tallest building in the country. And they made rock. Blackpool rock.

Blackpool rock is still made there to this day. Coronation Rock of Blackpool, whose rock is shown here, holds the world record for the largest stick of rock, weighing 424.5 kg and measuring 4.5 m long. ∎

Hot-water bottle

'Continental people have sex-lives; the English have hot-water bottles.' That was the view of the humorist George Mikes, who came to live in London from his native country, Hungary, in the 1930s.

Now, it is certainly true that there is nothing very sexy about a hot-water bottle, unless of course the smell of hot rubber gets you excited, but there is not much sexy about getting into a freezing cold bed either.

A hot-water bottle is a container filled with hot water and sealed with a screw-in stopper, used to provide warmth, usually in bed. In the event of injury it can also be held against a sore part of the body for pain relief.

Modern hot-water bottles have gone a bit soft, though. If you do not like to have hot rubber against your delicate skin you can get one covered in quilted fabric rather than the traditional ribbed rubber. And for the more gadget-minded there is now the gel-filled bottle which is heated in a microwave.

People used containers for warmth in bed in Britain as early as the 16th century. The earliest versions were metal and a maid or servant would fill the pan with hot coals from the embers of a log fire and place it in the bedclothes some time before their master or mistress was planning to retire to bed.

In the 1960s my father had a heavy pottery bottle, which he filled with hot water every night in winter. It worked fine back then, as his bed had sheets and blankets tucked in under the mattress, which held the bottle in place. He has moved on, like most British people, to using a loose duvet on his bed, so no longer uses the old bottle as it kept falling out of the bed and waking him up at night as it fell onto the wooden floor.

George Mikes made his original joke about the British attitude to sex and hot-water bottles in 1946 and, when asked about it in the 1970s, he agreed that things had moved on. But only because the English had discovered electric blankets since then. ∎

Continental people have sex-lives;

the English have hot-water bottles

Stinking Bishop cheese

There are 700 different cheeses in Britain, so trying to select just one to represent them all is hard. The obvious choice would be Cheddar since it accounts for half of all the cheese consumed in the country, and its origins are British, lying in the village of Cheddar in Somerset. The problem is that Cheddar is now so popular that it is made all over the world. It is the second most popular cheese in the USA, after mozzarella, for example. Or we could have selected one of the other regional cheeses – Red Leicester, Stilton, Wensleydale, Double Gloucester, Cornish Yarg, Caerphilly, Shropshire Blue, Lancashire, Cheshire – all of which have their own story to tell.

Instead we chose the wonderfully named Stinking Bishop, a cheese that has only wafted its way on to the British cheese scene within the last 40 years, and which is only made by one small dairy in Gloucestershire.

Voted Britain's smelliest cheese in 2009, the Press Association reported that 'the Stinking Bishop made by Charles Martell of Martell and Son in Gloucestershire blew the judges away and was described as smelling like a rugby club changing room.' Its creator

'Smelling like a rugby club changing room'

declared that he was 'thrilled and surprised to win' the award.

In spite of its name, Stinking Bishop does not actually taste anything like as pungent as it smells. Nor is it actually called Stinking Bishop because of its smell. It is a soft cheese whose rind is soaked every four weeks during the maturing process in a pear cider (or perry) made from the local Stinking Bishop pear. The pear is properly named Moorcroft, but was renamed after the man who bred it, a Mr Bishop, who was either reputed to have an ugly temper or to have a relaxed attitude to hygiene, depending on which source you believe. Its flavour has been variously described as sweetish, fruity and buttery.

In 2005 Stinking Bishop gained additional fame when it played a starring role in the Wallace & Gromit film, *The Curse of the Were-Rabbit*, in which it was used to revive Wallace, bringing him back from the dead.

Sales of Stinking Bishop rose fivefold after the film came out, no doubt due to its miraculous life-giving properties. ■

Marmite

Marmite is a thick, dark brown paste, with a strong, savoury flavour, usually eaten on toast or crumpets. Because of its powerful salty taste people usually spread it very thinly, so it is mostly sold in small jars. The name comes from the French word *marmite*, meaning a large cooking pot, a picture of which appears on the label. The jar itself is something of a design classic – distinctively shaped to resemble a casserole.

Made from yeast extract, Marmite is a by-product of beer brewing and so the first plant was sited alongside the Bass Brewery in Burton on Trent. Introduced in 1902, it was so popular that, just five years later, the then family-owned company opened a further plant in London.

Marmite is entirely vegetarian and it also contains many vitamins. You would think then that, in the age of ecological and health awareness, Marmite would tick all the right boxes: healthy, nutritious, does not involve cruelty to animals and makes use of a by-product that would otherwise be thrown away. But things are never that simple. In May 2010 the British press reported with indignation that the Danish government had banned Marmite precisely because it contains too many vitamins!

Facebook pages were set up and there were claims that British expats would stage protests or set up smuggling channels to import the product under cover. Seizing the opportunity for some publicity, a charity that campaigns for the rights of death-row prisoners even got in on the act, pointing out that whilst the Danish government was happy to permit the production in Denmark of a lethal drug exported to the USA for use on prisoners on death row, it banned a harmless substance like Marmite!

Constantly innovative, the manufacturers of Marmite leave no stone unturned in coming up with new Marmite-related ideas. In celebration of the Queen's Jubilee in 2012 many food manufacturers adapted their packaging to include the red, white and blue of the Union Jack flag. Marmite went one step further, renaming its product 'Ma'amite' for a limited period. It has also introduced a specially shaped knife (yes, called a Marmife) designed to help you get the very last bit of Marmite out of the jar. Also, 'Marmite Gold', which includes gold flecks, and 'Marmite XO', a specially matured variant with an even stronger taste, have been created.

Not all their ideas have been successful, though. In 2010 the manufacturer introduced a chocolate bar, 'Very Peculiar', combining milk chocolate with a little Marmite. A chef, asked to sample the chocolate, said of it, 'They have tried to make it as mild and sweet and innocuous as they can. It starts out as slightly bland... but, in the background, it is deeply nauseating.'

Because of its distinctive strong flavour people tend to either love or hate Marmite and the manufacturers have exploited its ability to polarise opinion by running marketing campaigns that play on the 'love it or hate it' theme. Marmite is now so entrenched in British life that the word Marmite is used generally to describe anything which people either love or hate. ■

More dangerous than a lethal drug used on death row?

Kendal Mint Cake

According to popular legend, the recipe for Kendal Mint Cake was originally discovered by accident.

A confectioner called Joseph Wiper who lived in Kendal, in Cumbria, was intending to make clear ('glacier') mints but took his eye off the cooking pan for a few minutes. When he looked back he noticed that the mixture had become cloudy. He poured it out into a tray and the result was Mint Cake. Wiper (who later emigrated to Canada) started making the Mint Cake at his small factory at Ferney Green in Kendal in 1869. Initially the product was only sold to locals but soon the railway encouraged sales further afield.

There was a second big break a few years later, in the early 20th century, when Kendal Mint Cake came to be prized as a concentrated source of energy much valued by explorers and mountaineers. The polar explorer Ernest Shackleton took it with him on his 1914–17 Transarctic Expedition and later Sir Edmund Hilary included it in the high altitude packs used on his 1953 ascent of Everest.

At the time of the Everest expedition Britain was still recovering from World War Two and sugar was in short supply, but staff at the factory gave up their own rations to allow the order to be fulfilled. This is still commemorated today on the back of packs of Romney's Kendal Mint Cake, where a member of the successful 1953 expedition is quoted as saying: 'It was easily the most popular item on our high altitude ration – our only criticism was that we did not have enough of it.'

Today, Kendal Mint Cake remains a popular energy source for walkers and is sold all over the country, but especially in the Lake District of north west England, the home of Kendal Mint Cake. ■

'It was easily the most popular item on our high altitude ration – our only criticism was that we did not have enough of it'

Policeman's helmet

Thirty years ago almost any newspaper report of police trying to deal with violent strikers or protesters would be accompanied by a photograph of a police officer having his helmet knocked from his head, its chinstrap hooked under the end of the unfortunate officer's nose.

The British police service dates back to 1829 when it was formed in London by Sir Robert Peel, and the early policemen came to be known as 'bobbies' or 'peelers'.

From the start they were unarmed, carrying only a wooden truncheon, together with a rattle and later a whistle in order to attract attention. The colour of their uniform – dark blue – was also selected to separate the police from the military, who typically wore red or, later, brown. Today British police only carry guns in extreme circumstances or at sensitive locations such as airports and embassies.

The design of the police helmet follows the form of the German *Pickelhaube*, the spiked helmet worn by German officers up to the time of World War One. Surprisingly, it has survived numerous moves to modernise the police uniform.

Today the traditional headgear of the policeman is reserved for officers patrolling the street (the 'bobby on the beat') and for obvious practical reasons it is replaced by a peaked cap for officers on mobile patrol in a car. Policemen charged with dealing with riots are now also better equipped, with purpose-made riot helmets and visors.

In the days when men and women almost always wore hats when going out, Britain was a centre of hat-making, but that industry has declined sharply, like many others. Now the police helmet is made by just two companies in Britain, Hobson in Essex and Christys in Oxfordshire, two survivors from the golden age of British hat-making. ∎

Follows the form of the German Pickelhaube

Comic seaside postcard

Picture postcards, reckoned to have been introduced by the Austrians in the 1860s, took some time to catch on in Britain. Government restrictions limited their use until the regulations were relaxed by a change in the law in 1902. They became so popular that the editor of a London newspaper predicted that 'in ten years Europe will be buried beneath picture postcards.'

Most of these cards were simple landscape views, but over the years the British comic postcard emerged. Such was its popularity that by the 1940s the idea of an English seaside resort without vulgar postcards was unimaginable.

Until the 1960s very few British people went abroad for their holidays. Instead most would head for the coast to one of the many seaside towns like Blackpool, Brighton or Skegness. By modern standards these were unsophisticated places, with guest houses run by fierce landladies who imposed severe rules on their long-suffering guests.

But there was still fun to be had and a break from repetitive factory life, which was the lot of most workers at the time. And the seaside postcard was part of that fun; the message you sent home to friends to assure them that you were having a great time, often in spite of the wet English climate. The heyday of the English seaside postcard

coincides with the peak in popularity of seaside resorts in the first half of the 20th century, so it went into decline in the 1960s and 70s, when British holidaymakers started heading for the more reliable climate of Spain or went in search of the gastronomic treats offered by France.

The survival of the comic English postcard into the 21st century is almost entirely due to one company, Bamforth of Yorkshire, who initiated comic postcards in the early 20th century and continue to produce them to this day.

The English seaside postcard may now look quaint, as it harks back to an age when sex was considered a bit naughty, and certainly not to be talked about in polite company. Many young, metropolitan sophisticates today probably do not even know that such cards still exist. Unless perhaps they had seen them at the Tate Gallery's 'Rude Britannia' exhibition in 2010, a show described by the BBC as a 'grand celebration of Britain's taste for the naughty but nice'.

As sexual attitudes have become more liberal, the frisson of childish naughtiness that is inseparable from these comic cards has largely been removed, but you will still find them bringing a smile on the seafronts of English seaside towns. ■

The English seaside postcard harks back to an age when sex was considered a bit naughty

Royal Ascot Ladies' Day hat

There has been horse racing at Ascot for over 300 years. The race course was established by Queen Anne in 1711 and the Gold Cup, a race for four-year-old horses, celebrated its 200th anniversary in 2007.

That race is the main event of Ladies' Day, and Ladies' Day is itself the highlight of the Royal Ascot racing meet, an event that is spread over five days in June – when fashion and Ascot hats come out in force.

Royal Ascot is the social event of the British racing and royal calendar. The crowds turn out, not just to watch the horse racing but to see the Queen and other members of the Royal Family at leisure, engaged in an activity that they enjoy. For visitors expecting to gain entry into the Royal Enclosure there is a very strict dress code. For ladies this specifies that: 'Dresses and skirts should be of modest length defined as falling just above the knee or longer... Hats should be worn; a headpiece which has a base of 4 in (10 cm) or more in diameter is acceptable as an alternative to a hat.'

The real spectacle of Royal Ascot is the fashion parade that is Ladies' Day. A hat is 'essential' even if you just plan to mix with the masses, and the hats ladies wear range from the elegant to the bizarre and flamboyant, usually the more outrageous the better. Ladies' Day at Royal Ascot is an opportunity for women of means to preen, be seen and if possible be photographed.

2011's event included a hat with tea cups, a blackberry tart, cherries and bunting perched precariously on top of a pale green brim. Another lady sported a model of the Titanic as her headpiece and several in one party wore hats adorned with different types of stuffed bird: pink flamingo, parrot, dove and black swan among them.

Hat designer Ilda Di Vico, pictured here, wore one of her own elaborate creations, a series of red and black hoops, with small ladybirds, worn stylishly down over the right eye.

By contrast the men tend to be much more conservative, but the occasional male is brave enough to join in the fun, like milliner David Shilling who appeared with two stuffed birds on the crown of his top hat. ■

Wearing a hat with tea cups, a blackberry tart, cherries and bunting perched precariously on top of a pale green brim

Morgan Three Wheeler

Morgan is a small, family-owned British manufacturer of very eccentric sports cars, most of which look as though they date back to the 1930s. At a time – over the last 20 years – when UK manufacturing in general has declined sharply, Morgan has gone from strength to strength. In 1990 it made just 400 cars, but by 2011 this had grown to 1,000 and its order book is still full, so it must be doing something right.

Its latest product, the Morgan Three Wheeler, illustrates the company's philosophy perfectly. On the one hand it harks back to the 1930s design that first made Morgan famous, but on the other it is a car that according to independent reviews is great fun to drive. No, it is probably not as safe as a conventional car, and no, you probably would not want to drive it to work every day. And, no, it is not as fast as a conventional sports car or hot hatchback; and, yes, it is rather expensive (at £30,000 or more) for a two-seater car that has no roof and is missing a wheel. But in spite of all that, customers are already queuing up to buy it, with first year production already sold out even before its formal launch in the USA.

The first Morgan was produced in 1910 and only went into production because of favourable response to its

design. That first car was also a three-wheeler, inspired as much by bicycle design as by cars. What made the Morgan Three Wheeler exceptional was its lightness, which made it unusually quick, rivalling many much more powerful cars. It was so fast that the Morgan won the 1913 French Grand Prix at Amiens, in spite of being the only three-wheeled car taking part.

Whilst the new Morgan Three Wheeler is, in many ways, a reinvention of the original, it also has some neatly quirky postmodern touches, for example, the starter button is the bomb release button from a Eurofighter jet. Buyers can choose paintwork in the style of a World War Two Spitfire, or of a hot rod, or they can opt to add decals of retro pin-ups in the style of a B-52 bomber. And it is also very quick, going from 0–60 in 4.5 seconds and having a top speed of more than 120 mph.

But what its customers love most is that, even at low speeds, it feels as though it is going fast. Like other design classics you do not buy a Morgan for its outright performance or for its practical value. You buy it because of the way it makes you feel. ■

Even at low speeds

it feels as though

it is going fast

The UK Sea Areas Map

The shipping forecast is an integral and reassuring part of life for many of the 10 million listeners to BBC Radio 4; so important, in fact, that it was included in the Opening Ceremony for the 2012 Olympic Games in London.

Broadcast four times a day, the shipping forecast is issued by the UK Meteorological (or Met) Office to provide vital weather information to shipping around the British coast. Sailors and fishermen depend on this forecast, and access to it on long-wave radio ensures that they can remain informed even if more modern systems such as radar, GPS and their own ship-to-shore radio should fail.

Key to its understanding is the Sea Areas map which shows the location of the individual zones around Britain, and an understanding of where they are adds to the strange pleasure that many derive from the Shipping Forecast itself. Of course, neither you nor most of the other listeners need to know what the weather conditions are like in the North Sea west of Norway (that would be in sea areas North Utsire or South Utsire), but that is not the point. As you snuggle under your bedclothes to stay warm in the early hours of a sleepless night it will greatly add to your pleasure to know that it is blowing a Force 9 gale in Southeast Iceland.

Starting in the north east with Viking, the newsreader will take you on a tour of Britain, through Dogger, Fisher, German Bight and Portland, across Fitzroy (named after the British pioneer of weather forecasting) and up around Ireland, finishing in Hebrides, Bailey and Fair Isle, Faeroes and Southeast Iceland.

The interest that many British people have in the shipping forecast reflects the fascination that the ever-changing British weather seems to hold for us. Any overseas visitor to Britain can be assured that the weather is a perfect subject with which to initiate casual conversation. The British tend to be rather reserved and have to have a good reason to talk to one another, and the weather, often very changeable in Britain, can provide the perfect excuse. So it is perfectly acceptable for someone to go into a shop or pub and address a complete stranger with an observation about the weather, something simple like 'Lovely day' or on a rainy day in August: 'Whatever happened to the summer they promised us?' ■

As you snuggle under your bedclothes it will greatly add to your pleasure to know that it is blowing a Force 9 gale in South East Iceland

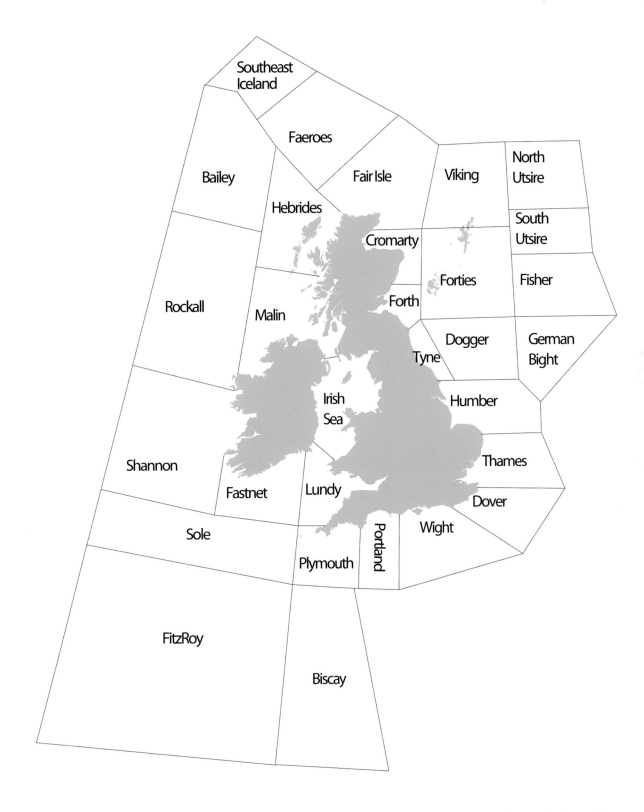

Southeast Iceland

Faeroes

Fair Isle

Viking

North Utsire

Bailey

Hebrides

Cromarty

South Utsire

Rockall

Malin

Forth

Forties

Fisher

Dogger

German Bight

Tyne

Shannon

Fastnet

Lundy

Irish Sea

Humber

Thames

Sole

Plymouth

Portland

Wight

Dover

FitzRoy

Biscay

Deck chair

The deck chair is a masterpiece of elegant design, simple in concept, cheap to make, easy to store and comfortable to sit in. Constructed from as few as 11 pieces of wood, a straight length of fabric and a handful of fastenings, the deck chair provides a comfortable and relaxing way to enjoy the sunshine on a warm summer's afternoon, especially on a beach by the sea.

Folding chairs were recorded in Egyptian times, but it was in the late 19th century that the modern deck chair became popular. John Thomas Moore patented his design for a folding chair in 1886. As the name 'deck chair' suggests, it was popular for sitting out on the deck of an ocean liner as it transported its passengers to various parts of the then flourishing British Empire. It also became

associated with the healthy sea air enjoyed on deck, and its light weight and compact dimensions when folded made it ideal for storage on a ship.

The deck chair was soon adopted on beaches and piers around Britain's coastline. Once again it scored because it was comfortable and easy to fold away for storage at the end of the day or over the winter.

Its popularity peaked with the heyday of the British seaside holiday – up to the 1950s – before British people started going abroad to find more reliable sunshine, but even now it is easy to hire a deck chair by the hour or the day, not just at the seaside (Brighton is reputed to have some 3,000 deck chairs) but also in many London parks.

The deck chair has also found its way into a common phrase. If someone tells you a proposed activity is like 'rearranging the deck chairs on the Titanic' you will know that they mean that they think it is too trivial to help deal with the real crisis. ■

Popular for sitting out on the deck of an ocean liner as it transported its passengers to various parts of the flourishing British Empire

'Folk the Banks' T-shirt

In 2008 the British banking system, like many others around the world, came close to collapse, destroyed by the over-availability of credit and the recklessness of its bankers. And because London is such a prominent centre of global finance it felt the fallout even more intensely than elsewhere. When the Occupy Wall Street movement gained prominence in New York, groups in London were quick to follow suit, taking up their protest on the edge of the City of London outside St Paul's Cathedral.

Reprising his role as the graphic art leader of the anti-establishment movement was Jamie Reid, whose cover for a fund-raising music album titled 'Folk the Banks' was quickly taken up as a T-shirt design. Reid has been here before, almost 40 years ago...

In the mid 1970s pop music in Britain was largely split between the earnest post-hippy rock groups like Pink Floyd or Led Zeppelin and the glam rock scene of T Rex and David Bowie. But in 1976 a new musical force punched its way into the headlines: Punk. Led by the Sex Pistols, punk was the complete opposite of mainstream music; it was disrespectful, ugly, foul-mouthed, angry, discordant and nihilistic.

At the heart of this anarchistic force was the graphic artist Jamie Reid. He designed all the covers for the most famous Pistols records, and they perfectly captured the spirit of the time. Reid took establishment images like the Queen's head and defaced them, adding lettering cut from newspapers to create the effect of a ransom note – precisely the aggressive and beyond-the-law values that the Sex Pistols wanted to be known for.

Though it is now more than 30 years since the Sex Pistols scandalised respectable British middle class parents (and delighted their rebellious teenage children), they remain a potent symbol of outrage, and you can still buy the Reid-designed T-shirts bearing the cover design of their one studio album, *Never Mind the Bollocks*.

If punk personified Britain in the 1970s then it is the greed of bankers and the ensuing banking crisis that have characterised the first decade of the 21st century. True to his principles, Jamie Reid continues to use his unique style of collage to produce art that challenges the establishment. It is hard to imagine Reid selling out like Sex Pistols lead singer Johnny Rotten, who capitalised on his fame by appearing on celebrity reality TV show *I'm a Celebrity... Get Me Out of Here!* and later by advertising butter on television.

When Occupation Records first launched its crowd-funded album of protest folk music, 'Folk the Banks', Reid was the natural choice to design its cover. The music may not have the raw power of punk and there may not be the publicity force of Malcolm McLaren to drive it as there was with punk, but the raw anger is still there. We have yet to see whether the 'Folk the Banks' T-shirt will enjoy the longevity of the Sex Pistols' *Never Mind the Bollocks*. ▪

Hard to imagine Jamie Reid selling out to advertise butter on television

Twenty pound note

The twenty pound note is one of the three paper notes in widest circulation in Britain: if you change another currency into sterling then the chances are you will receive your pounds in £5, £10, £20 and £50 notes, although larger ones do exist. If you are one of the super-rich you can even aspire to owning a 'Titan', which is a million pound bank note, of which there are only 40 in existence (but before you get too excited you should note that Titans are only used within the banking system and are not obtainable by the general public).

The first notes in pounds sterling were issued in 1696, making sterling the world's oldest currency still in use. Until 1971 the pound was divided into 20 shillings, each shilling equalling 12 old pence, but in 1971 the current decimal system was introduced, greatly simplifying things. So one pound now is made up of 100 new pence. The pound – along with the US Dollar, the Euro and the Japanese Yen – is one of the four most commonly traded currencies and the third most commonly held currency in global reserves.

The twenty pound note was introduced in 1745 but was discontinued during World War Two due to fears of a German attempt to issue fake currency, and it was only reintroduced thirty years later, in 1970.

All sterling notes show the picture of the reigning monarch on one side and a historical figure on the

Sterling is the world's oldest currency still in use

back. As Queen Elizabeth II has been on the British throne since 1953 all current bank notes show her head on the front side.

The custom of depicting historical figures on the reverse of banknotes began with the image of William Shakespeare being used on the £20 note in 1970. Since then, many other famous Britons have featured on successive issues. Others who have appeared on the £20 note include Michael Faraday (the English chemist and physicist best known for his experiments on electromagnetism) and Edward Elgar (the composer best known for works such as the Enigma Variations).

The current twenty pound note carries the portrait of Adam Smith, commonly credited as the father of modern economics and for many the father of capitalism itself. Smith's most famous work is *The Wealth of Nations* in which he championed the cause of free trade, arguing that if Country A can make a product more cheaply than Country B then it is better for B to buy from A and concentrate on making those things in which it has a competitive advantage.

It may be devotion to this concept of free trade that explains why so many everyday British icons are now owned by foreign companies, when other countries seem to fight hard to retain control of their national brands. ■

A–Z street map

The first A–Z street map was created by Phyllis Pearsall in 1935. Legend has it that she was trying to find her way to a party in the London district of Belgravia, armed with the latest map she could find. But, as that map was more than 15 years old she got lost and never got there.

The legend continues that, spurred by this experience, Phyllis decided to make a completely new map of London. To do this she would get up at 5 a.m. every day, working for up to 18 hours a day, mapping and indexing every one of London's 23,000 streets and walking a total of 3,000 miles.

At the end of this labour, however, she was unable to persuade any of the existing book publishers to take her book on so decided to publish it herself by founding the Geographers' Map Company.

She published *The A–Z Atlas and Guide to London and Suburbs* in 1936 and today almost anyone who lives in London will have a recent copy on their bookshelf.

This legend has however sadly been called into doubt by recent researchers who point out that the A–Z was not the first documented map of London and that they actually existed as far back as the 17th century. They also point out that Phyllis's father had himself previously set up a mapping company so this was not quite the pioneering venture it sounds. As for the claims about the distance she walked they point out that much of the information would have been available at borough town halls. The legend is much more interesting, though, so we'll stick with that. ■

Legend has it that Phyllis Pearsall walked a total of 3,000 miles to create the first A–Z of London

Front cover image used with the knowledge and permission of Geographers' A-Z Map Co. Ltd

Union Jack cushion

The British flag, known as the Union Jack or Union Flag, is one of the most distinctive national flags in the world. The current layout dates back to 1801, to the Union of Great Britain and Ireland.

The design is distinctive because it was created by combining the national flags of Scotland, England and Ireland: the white diagonal cross of Saint Andrew on its blue background for Scotland, the red vertical cross of Saint George for England and the red diagonal cross of Saint Patrick for Ireland. Although Wales is also one of the four kingdoms making up Great Britain, it is not represented in the current design of the Union Jack. This omission was raised in Parliament in 2007 by a Labour MP and the government is reported to be looking at a suitable way of including the Welsh flag, which consists of a red dragon on a green and white background, into the Union Jack.

Meanwhile some in Scotland are keen on pushing for independence, so the Union Jack could change completely beyond recognition over the coming years.

One reason for the enduring iconic status of the Union Jack is its association with youth culture and fashion. At the height of Beatlemania in the early 1960s London's Carnaby Street became a focal point for post-war exuberance. Musicians adopted the Union Jack, notably Pete Townsend, who wore a Union Jack jacket on The Who's first album cover, and later the punks who wore Vivienne Westwood Union Jack T-shirts in the 1970s. Freddie Mercury, Oasis and the Spice Girls have all given further exposure to the design.

Today you can find the Union Jack on all kinds of clothing and home accessories, including bedding, mugs, teapots and cushions. And to add a touch of style to your kitchen attire when demonstrating your cooking skills, why not try a Union Jack apron? ■

The Union Jack could change beyond recognition over the coming years

Hot cross bun

A hot cross bun is a sweet spiced bun made with raisins and candied fruits, traditionally only made in the run-up to Easter, but increasingly available at other times of year as well. The cross on the top symbolises the crucifixion of Christ, which is why the hot cross bun was traditionally associated with Good Friday, when the buns would be cut in half and eaten either cold or toasted, usually with butter.

In spite of their strong links to Christianity, some believe that people were making hot cross buns long before the religion came to Britain. They are certainly now a well-established tradition, even featuring in a childrens' nursery rhyme:

Hot cross buns,
Hot cross buns,
One ha' penny,
Two ha' penny,
Hot cross buns.

If you have no daughters,
Give them to your sons,
One ha' penny,
Two ha' penny,
Hot cross buns.

There are also superstitions associated with hot cross buns. For example, one of them says that a hot cross bun baked on Good Friday will not go mouldy during the subsequent year.

In London there is a pub called The Widow's Son, where a woman once lived whose son was due home on leave from the Royal Navy. Expecting him home on Good Friday, she was heartbroken when he did not arrive. Living in hope, she would bake a new bun for him every Easter, adding to those she had kept from previous years. When she died these buns were found hanging from a beam in her cottage, and ever since the pub was opened in 1848 the tradition has been maintained by each subsequent landlord. ■

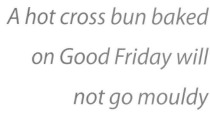

A hot cross bun baked on Good Friday will not go mouldy

Orange marmalade

Every January, in the midst of the grey, gloomy days of a British winter, chunky, shiny-skinned oranges appear on greengrocers' shelves all over the country. They stay for just a few short weeks and are gone. These are not the usual sweet oranges that you can find at any time of the year; these are Seville oranges. And whilst they can be used in a number of dishes, their bitter flavour makes them perfect for one purpose above all others: making marmalade.

You may wonder how a product using Spanish oranges could come to be associated with Britain at all, but so great is the demand for these oranges for marmalade production that almost all the Seville oranges grown in Andalucia in southern Spain are now shipped to Britain.

It is said that marmalade-making in Britain started in Scotland, though different forms of marmalade had been produced earlier in other countries. It comes from the Portuguese word, marmelo, meaning quince, but these earlier marmalades had the consistency of a paste, unlike the chunky texture of modern-day marmalade.

According to legend, a ship carrying Seville oranges had to seek refuge from a storm in the harbour at Dundee. Fearing the loss of his cargo due to the

delay, the shipowner put the oranges up for sale at a bargain price and they were snapped up by a local grocer, James Keiller. Some say he thought he was buying sweet oranges and was dismayed when he discovered that he had bought bitter Sevilles. Undeterred his wife Janet added large quantities of sugar to sweeten the oranges and included the cooked peel in the finished preserve, creating marmalade as we know it today. In 1797 Keiller opened his first factory and so began Dundee's long association with marmalade.

Other companies were quick to pick up the idea of marmalade production and the two leading UK brands are Frank Cooper's Oxford Marmalade and the family-owned Wilkin's Tiptree Marmalade. You will find their preserves in hotels and restaurants all over the world, but their marmalade is really an integral part of an English breakfast, rounding off the best meal of the day.

In *From Russia With Love*, Ian Fleming wrote that breakfast, including toast, butter and orange marmalade, was James Bond's favourite meal of the day.

Marmalade has accompanied British travellers from explorers to travel writers and politicians, who share a reluctance to venture forth without the family palate-waking sweet/bitter combination of marmalade. Visit small towns, gift shops or village fetes around Britain and the chances are you will find jars of home-made marmalade on sale, all offering an unpredictable twist on this British favourite. Will it be hard and chunky, or so liquid that you struggle to balance it on your toast? Finding out is one of the small but enjoyable pleasures of travelling round Britain. ∎

Almost all the Seville oranges gathered in Andalusia are shipped to Britain

Royal Worcester wedding mug

When Prince Charles married Lady Diana Spencer in 1981, 600,000 people crowded the streets of London to catch a glimpse of them. Another 750 million worldwide watched their wedding on television.

Thirty years later a million people lined the route taken by Charles' son William when he married Kate Middleton and as many as two billion people worldwide were reckoned to have caught the event on TV or via the internet. That's almost one in three people on the planet.

The technology may have been transformed in the period between 1981 and 2011, but the romance of British royalty, far from diminishing, as you might have expected in more egalitarian times, has only increased, fuelled by our universal mania for celebrity.

The fascination that British royalty holds for people all over the world is unrivalled. Perhaps the odd Hollywood couple – Angelina and Brad, perhaps – could compete. But would people buy memorabilia to capture the event? It seems unlikely somehow.

Royal Worcester, who made the mug shown here, dates back to 1751, making it one of the oldest remaining English pottery brands still in existence. Its royal wedding collection, 'crafted from fine bone china and finished in 22 carat gold' included a pill box, a loving cup (a cup with two handles) and a lion-head vase.

Not all the commemorative goods on sale in the run-up to the Royal Wedding were so concerned with maintaining dignity or respect. On offer elsewhere was Katea, teabags with pictures of the royal couple. For those disgusted by the whole event graphic designer Lydia Leith offered a commemorative sick bag. Another company, Crown Jewels, tastefully packaged up some royal wedding condoms, and Nottingham's Castle Rock Brewery produced bottles of beer under the label 'Kiss Me Kate'.

Spare a thought though for the poor man who designed one Royal Wedding mug – the star of many news reports at the time – which included a picture of Kate Middleton together with not her husband-to-be, but her future brother-in-law, Prince Harry. We hope the maker used the publicity to sell his whole stock as a future classic. ■

Almost one in three people on the planet watched the event on TV or via the internet

Rugby ball

Named after Rugby School (itself located in the town of Rugby), the traditional story is that rugby was invented in 1823 when a player named William Webb Ellis ignored the rules of football, picked up the ball and ran with it. Though the evidence for this story is weak, the international rugby committee has named the Rugby World Cup the William Webb Ellis Trophy, demonstrating that one should never allow strict historical accuracy to get in the way of a good story.

In the 19th century the technology for making both football and rugby balls was primitive by any standards. Footballs were supposed to be spherical, but rarely were in practice. One reason for this was that they were made using a pig's bladder encased in stitched leather, so the shape of the ball was dictated by the shape of the bladder and the evenness of the stitching.

Two people, Richard Lindon and William Gilbert, both boot and shoemakers and both located close to the gates of Rugby School, led the way in making the balls. Richard Lindon's wife, in addition to bearing him 17 children, also helped him make the balls. Her role was to blow them up using a small clay pipe and her own lung power. This proved to be very hazardous, as the pig's bladders often carried germs which could cause life-threatening diseases. It is said that Mrs Lindon herself died prematurely from such a disease (though after a lifetime spent blowing up rugby balls and bearing 17 children you might wonder if she died from simple exhaustion). Motivated by her loss, Lindon developed a new system using a rubber bladder and a brass pump, which removed the danger. He never patented this new

process, which not only made balls easier to blow up, but also provided greater control over the shape of the ball.

Probably the greatest contribution the British made to the development of sports like football and rugby was to introduce standard rules, so that teams from different parts of the country or of the world could compete on the same basis. This simple innovation took many years of adaptation to achieve, and it sometimes led to splits in the sport. That is why today we have two types of rugby – Rugby Union and Rugby League – which are played to different rules. The original split, which took place in 1895, was focused on the question of whether players should be compensated for taking time off work to play in matches, some arguing that this was necessary for low paid manual workers, whilst others (mainly the better off) felt it would compromise the amateur ethos of the sport.

The same process of standardisation was brought to bear on the shape and size of the rugby football. The original pig's bladder balls tended to be plum-shaped but after 1870, with the introduction of the rubber bladder, they became more egg-shaped to aid handling. In 1892 the Rugby Football Union decided that the ball must be oval and the gradual flattening of the ball continued over the years. Despite the application of fish oil and animal fat, the leather-encased balls were prone to water-logging, but it was not until the 1980s that leather was finally replaced by waterproof synthetics. ∎

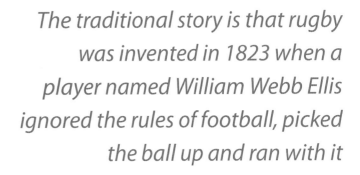

The traditional story is that rugby was invented in 1823 when a player named William Webb Ellis ignored the rules of football, picked the ball up and ran with it

Christmas pudding

Christmas pudding is sometimes called plum pudding, even though it usually contains no plums at all. The main ingredients are flour, raisins, sultanas, currants, suet, mixed spices, dark sugars and various forms of alcohol, such as beer, brandy and rum.

Plum pudding is usually served with sweet brandy butter or cream, and tends to be very rich. This is not a dish for the faint-hearted, especially if they have already eaten a generous portion of turkey, accompanied by roast potatoes, vegetables, stuffing and bread sauce or gravy immediately before it.

It is a strange thing, the Christmas pudding; it originally contained meat (it still normally contains suet, which makes it unsuitable for vegetarians), which was stored with dry fruits to help preserve it after the autumn slaughter of livestock. As methods of preserving meat improved, however, the meat disappeared from the recipe and the fruit and sugar content increased. (Mince pies also evolved in the same way, but in the latter case the name stuck – even though the mince pie, like the Christmas pudding, now contains no meat.)

The Christmas pudding can be traced back to medieval times when the Church declared that each household should prepare a pudding that should include 13 ingredients, to represent Christ and the 12 apostles. It was also traditional that every member of the household should stir the pudding, making a wish at the same time. In richer households the cook would include silver coins into the pudding, making a wish at the same time. An alternative to this coin was the Christmas pudding charm. Made from silver or porcelain, you can still buy these charms today. Typically they take the form of a button, a wishbone, a bird, a coin or a horseshoe. Whoever finds the charm will be blessed with good fortune – provided of course that they have not swallowed it by mistake.

Cooks would typically prepare the pudding several weeks in advance and would then hang it in a cloth to mature, before steaming it for two hours immediately before serving.

The final touch for the perfectly served Christmas pudding is to turn the lights down low and then pour brandy over it and set it alight. And as the final mouthful slips joyfully down your throat, you can start to think about your New Year's diet... ■

As the final mouthful slips joyfully down your throat, you can start to think about your New Year's diet

Fish and chips

Even if you are a vegetarian, you should at least once try savouring the distinctive smell of British fish and chips – even if you do not eat any. For everyone else fish and chips should be eaten topped with a dash of salt and a splash of vinegar, ideally while walking along a seafront – the authentic British seaside experience.

The first fish and chip shop opened in Britain in 1860, and fish and chips quickly became the unrivalled British takeaway food – the first fast food to be offered in this country. By the 1930s there were 35,000 fish and chip shops in the UK. Fish and chips was one of just a small number of foods not to be rationed during the Second World War. It was then, and still is, a popular meal for families to have at home, or when travelling to the seaside for a day out. Today, even though the number of fish and chip shops has fallen to just 10,000 outlets, they still sell almost a quarter of all the white fish consumed in the United Kingdom, and a tenth of all the potatoes.

You do not have to go far in any British town to find one. Fish and chip shops are usually easy to spot with their brightly lit signs and a tendency (shared with British hairdressers) to come up with punning names like The Codfather, The Plaice to be, The Frying Scotsman, Frying Nemo, A Salt N Battered, and even In Cod We Trust.

The decline in the number of fish and chip shops on the streets of Britain is not so much because the British have stopped enjoying fish and chips; more that they now have much more choice. Chinese and Indian takeaways first became widespread in the 1960s. Today the nation's single favourite dish is not fish and chips but chicken tikka masala. If you then add in all the other competition from burger, fried chicken, pizza and kebab shops, then you can see why fish and chip shops are no longer quite the force they once were. The alternatives offer quick food, often at prices that a fish and chip shop selling the best fresh fish simply cannot match.

However, all is not lost. Whilst there are still many places where you will be served a greasy stack of soggy battered fish on a mound of slippery soft chips, a new breed of fish and chip shops is emerging. Fish and chip shops are fighting back with high quality fresh fish at prices which customers are willing to queue for. (One successful takeaway has even set up a webcam so that its customers can go online to check how long the queue outside their shop is.) Others have started to experiment with alternatives to the usual cod, plaice and haddock, offering more unusual seafood like calamari and mackerel, along with new flavours of batter such as massala, lemon, lime and chilli. ∎

Punning names like

The Codfather,

The Plaice to be,

Frying Nemo

and In Cod We Trust

King James Bible

Some objects are appealing because they have clearly been designed with flair, because they look, feel or smell enticing. Or because they just look right. Others have less immediate impact. These are the objects whose cultural significance relates more to their content than to aesthetics, and they can often take longer to be truly appreciated.

The King James Bible – sometimes called the Authorised Version – is a book that took seven years and 47 scholars to write and has had 400 years to mature and be appreciated. Begun in 1604 and completed 1611, it has been described as the only great work of art ever to be created by a committee.

Although 400 years old, the King James Bible can claim to be a contemporary object because it continues to influence even those who are not Christians. The fact that it remains in print to this day, that it is still revered even after several attempts at creating more modern tellings of Bible stories bears testimony to its continuing cultural significance.

To understand the importance of the King James Bible you need only look at the number of phrases still in use

in everyday English that come from it. Take for example: a labour of love; a bird in the hand is worth two in the bush; a leopard cannot change its spots; eat, drink and be merry; forbidden fruit; white as snow and so on.

According to the 2001 census, 72 per cent of the British population described themselves as Christians, 16 per cent had no religion, almost 3 per cent were Muslim, 1 per cent Hindu, the remaining 8 per cent being a mix of Sikh, Jewish, Buddhist, Druid and other religions including a very small minority of self-proclaimed Jedis.

However, no one could seriously claim that almost three quarters of the British population are practising Christians. British society is more secular than ever before. A 2007 survey showed that only 10 per cent of the population attend church weekly and two thirds had not gone to church in the last year. Not just that, but the average age of churchgoers is increasing, suggesting that the young are not being drawn in by any of the Christian churches, including the Church of England.

Church attendance certainly increases around Christmas, with church pews that are empty most of the year packed with families who enjoy singing Christmas carols. In spite of the decline in church attendance the King James Bible still stands as a British icon, its poetry and language continuing to exercise an unseen and under-recognised influence. ∎

A labour of love

Lyle's Golden Syrup

Imagine you are a sugar maker and have just come up with a great new product – a sweet golden syrup, which your first customers have taken up with great enthusiasm. So now you ask your marketing people to come up with a label and brand image to go with it. What do they propose? A picture of a dead lion whose carcass has been invaded by bees. Accompanied by a quote from the Bible. Improbable as it may sound, you have just created a brand image that will last for over 120 years and be recognised by the Guinness Book of Records as the longest established brand in the world.

In 1881 Abram Lyle set up a sugar refinery and a couple of years later noticed that the sugar cane refining process produced a treacly sort of syrup, which could be further refined. The result was a preserve and sweetener for cooking. He started selling small quantities of 'Goldie' from wooden casks to his employees and local customers. Word spread quickly, and soon Lyle was selling a tonne a week. He replaced the wooden casks with 'Lyle's Golden Syrup' dispensers, and they soon began to appear on the shelves of grocery stores all over London.

In 1904 the 'lion and bees' image was registered as Lyle's trademark, and it appears on the tin to this day. The design came, not from an advertising agency but from Abram Lyle himself: it refers to a story in the Old Testament, in which Samson killed a lion, then saw that bees had formed a honeycomb in the lion's carcass. The words from the Bible still appear on the tin today: 'Out of the strong came forth sweetness'.

One of the marks of a successful British company has been that it becomes an official supplier to the Royal Family, an accolade that is marked by the granting of a Royal warrant. A supplier who gains the Royal warrant is entitled to show it on its product packaging. Whilst this may not carry quite the same weight today as it did in the past, it still adds a touch of class to your label. Tate & Lyle gained a royal warrant for its golden syrup in 1922 and, as you might expect, it remains on the tin to this day.

Golden syrup may be used in cooking or eaten spread on toast. But an ideal way to sample it is by ordering one of the most popular desserts on British pub menus: Treacle Pudding – with custard, of course. ■

A sweet syrup promoted using a picture of a dead lion whose carcass has been invaded by bees

Oyster card

The Oyster card was introduced in London in 2003 and there are now more than 34 million in use, with 80 per cent of journeys made on London transport using it. To Londoners it is an everyday object, as banal as a credit card, but to anyone visiting the city for the first time – and unaccustomed to it – the Oyster card can seem part of a baffling system that sends you rushing to the nearest taxi rank.

If you plan to stay in London for more than just a few days, you will save money if you get an Oyster card. The same size as a standard credit card, the Oyster allows you to travel on London overground trains, buses and on the tube at the lowest available cost. Once you have it, you will no longer have to queue to buy a ticket; you simply top it up every now and then and hold it over a card reader as you enter the train or bus.

Why is it called an Oyster card? It seems that Transport for London, who operate the system, wanted to play on the idea of the oyster as a shell that is safe and contains something valuable (the pearl being a microchip embedded inside the card). It also picks up on the saying: 'the world is your oyster', in this case the key to unlocking the many hidden gems in the city. ■

The world is your oyster

Railway station sign

If you want to find your way to the railway station in any town or city in Britain, then look out for the symbol shown here, two opposite-facing arrows set on two parallel lines.

This design was created in 1965 as a logo for British Rail, the nationalised rail system at that time. Even though British Rail was broken up in the 1990s and is now operated by a number of separate companies, the logo remains. One reason for its continued use is that it is a simple and elegant representation of the railway system – the parallel lines evoking the railway tracks and the two interlocking arrows representing trains passing one another, one heading east, the other west.

The design was created by a graphic designer called Gerald Burney, who worked for a design consultancy called the Design Research Unit and his graphic has outlived the early criticism it received.

The British railway system has been the butt of many jokes over the years, gaining a reputation for late trains and dry, taste-free sandwiches. So, it is maybe not so surprising that Burney's new design came in for its own share of criticism. Some commentators complained about the loss of the lion crest on the previous British Railways flag, while others contemptuously compared the design to a piece of 'barbed wire'. But the fact is that the symbol has survived, even though the unloved organisation it represented has long gone. A tribute to the effectiveness of this deceptively simple design. ∎

Some compared the design to a piece of barbed wire

Tartan kilt

Writing in *The Independent* newspaper recently, the former British ambassador to Uzbekhistan, Craig Murray observed that he generally received a warm welcome wherever he went wearing his kilt. It is, after all, a universally recognised symbol of Scotland, and in the wake of the film *Braveheart* Scotland is seen by many as a romantic kingdom of poet warriors. But Murray acknowledged that the kilt had also on occasion caused him problems. He was nearly thrown out of a bar in Tashkent by staff wary of a man wearing a skirt, and a police commander at a wedding in Ghana gently pointed out to him that homosexuality was illegal in that country, recommending that he act with greater discretion in future.

The kilt is a knee-length skirt-like garment, with pleats at the back, mostly associated today with Scotland, with variants found in other Celtic traditions including Wales and Ireland. It has no pockets so it is typically worn with a sporran, a pouch which hangs at the front of the kilt. It dates back at least to the 16th century and the word may derive from the Old Norse kjalta.

As for the tartan, the earliest example in Scotland dates from the 3rd century AD – found stuffed into the top of a pot containing Roman coins.

The tartan kilt is – along with the bagpipes – the most visible physical symbol of Scottish identity. In the past that strong association has lead to it being banned because of fears held by King George II of the threat posed by warrior highland clans. In 1746 a 'Dress Act' was passed banning kilts, with severe penalties for those breaking the law, but the ban only lasted 35 years, and when King George IV visited Scotland in 1822, himself wearing a kilt, the fashion for kilt-wearing, which continues to this day, was firmly established.

Today the kilt is generally only worn on special occasions – celebrations like weddings, Hogmanay (the welcoming of the New Year) or a ceilidh (a traditional dance with folk music). A good kilt, together with the accompanying jacket, sporran, hose, brogues and accessories can cost you over £1,000, but with care can last a lifetime.

If you want you can even specify a more fashionable kilt outfit such as the Pure White fashion kilt (white kilt with white jacket, white sporran and white accessories) or the similar Soft Gold. Only for the brave of heart. ▪

Once banned, now a universal symbol of Scotland

Red Nose

It was not until 1988 that the red nose gained its independence. Until that time it had always been attached to the face of a living being, whether it was Rudolph, the red-nosed reindeer pulling Santa Claus's sleigh on Christmas Day, or someone suffering from a severe cold.

In 1988 all that changed with the arrival of the first Comic Relief Red Nose Day, a charity fundraising event that has taken place every two years ever since. The charity Comic Relief was formed in 1985 and initially consisted of one-off TV programmes and appeals. It was the creation of Red Nose Day that really put it on the map, bringing together sponsorship money, fundraising activities by members of the public, and straight donations to the charity. All of this is focused on a single all-evening TV programme hosted by the BBC in March each second year. Such is its popularity that it attracted 10 million viewers in 2011, equivalent to one in six people in Britain.

The Comic Relief Red Nose is given away in exchange for a donation and has taken on many forms over the years. Initially it was simply a shiny red hollow plastic sphere with a slit at the back to fit over your nose. In 1991 it grew a couple of small arms. A couple of years later it morphed into a tomato, complete with a green stem, and in 1995 it was heat-sensitive, changing colour with the temperature. It has continued to evolve, going fluffy and getting various faces. 2003's nose featured spikey hair, which when worn upside down, looked like a moustache.

By 2011 the Red Nose had become the three distinct Monster noses shown here: Captain Conk with a pirate's eye patch and skull and crossbones scarf, Honkus with a broad mouth and piranha-like teeth and finally the more nerdy Chucklechomp, wearing glasses.

If you want to take part but do not fancy wearing a nose yourself you can buy one to fit on the front of your car. (You will probably see some whose owners never get around to removing them and leave them on all year.)

Over the years over 60 million noses have been sold, contributing to the mind-boggling sums raised by Comic Relief for charities all over the world. In 1988 the charity raised £15 million. By 2011 this had grown to over £100 million. ∎

In 1988 the red nose gained its independence

Pub sign

The pub (short for public house) remains the social centre of many communities in Britain. The oldest pub today, according to *The Guinness Book of Records*, is Ye Olde Fighting Cockes in St Albans, which can trace its history back almost a thousand years.

But the pub is under threat. The number of them has fallen in recent years: a report in 2010 claimed that more than 50 pubs a week were closing and that the number of pubs had dropped from 69,000 in 1980 to 52,000 now. That is still one pub for every 12,000 people, though, and in some communities where the pub was threatened with closure, its customers have taken it over. For example, when the villagers of Crosby Ravensworth in Cumbria heard that their pub was to close they got together and raised enough money to buy and run it as a co-operative, with investors attracted from as far away as Alaska and Australia.

Since 1393 all pubs have been obliged by law to carry a pub sign:

'Whosoever shall brew ale in the town with intention of selling it must hang out a sign, otherwise he shall forfeit his ale.'

The idea behind the law was to make sure that official inspectors – charged with ensuring that the quality of the beer on sale was acceptable – could visually identify all the pubs with ease. In practice this also proved to be a great marketing idea, as a pub sign with a picture could be easily identified even by those who could not read.

The pub sign remains an important landmark to this day, usually hanging from the front of the pub or from a pole by the roadside. Pubs have often changed their names to pick up on events like battles or military

'Whosoever shall brew ale in the town with intention of selling it must hang out a sign'

leaders (The Lord Nelson) or local activities such as trades (The Bricklayers' Arms) or sports (The Cricketers' Arms) or after the reigning monarch (the pub in the BBC soap opera Eastenders is the Queen Victoria, known to its patrons as The Queen Vic). Some reflect their times – The Coach & Horses would probably date from the 18th century and be on one of the early main roads, while The Railway Inn would have been built a century or more later.

There is a story that, in Stony Stratford, mid-way on the journey between London and the Midlands, the London coach would change horses at a pub named The Bull, and the Birmingham coach across the road would stop at The Cock Inn. The passengers from each coach would swap news while waiting for the change, and it is from this that the phrase 'cock and bull story' (meaning a ridiculous and unbelievable story) is said to have originated.

The pub continues to evolve so though their numbers may continue to fall, they will certainly not disappear. Some time ago, the typical pub was a smoky and unsophisticated place serving drinks (mainly room-temperature bitter) to mainly male customers. Now most successful pubs serve food – often to gourmet standards. Smoking is banned by law and the ambience now much more family-friendly. ∎

Bottle of Bitter & Twisted beer

Old Thumper, Hobgoblin, Fursty Ferret, Waggle Dance, Bruins Ruin, Piddle in the Hole: just some of the strange and playful names of beers that you can find on any supermarket shelf in Britain. Together they tell a story of the recent renaissance of British beer-making after many years of sad decline.

The beer bottle shown here, Harviestoun Brewery's award-winning Bitter & Twisted is a case in point. This Scottish brewery was started in 1984 by Ken Brooker, who had previously worked for the Ford Motor Company for over 20 years. ('Bitter and twisted' is a term used to describe someone who is irritable and disgruntled – and the beer was named by Ken's wife as a reference to him.) One of their other beers is a dark stout beer (also shown here), which Ken named Old Engine Oil, as its colour reminded him of the black oil drained from the sump of a car.

Together with a friend, Ken started the brewery on a farm in Scotland, and in 2007 their efforts were rewarded when Bitter & Twisted was named 'World's Best Ale' at the World Beer Awards. Breweries like Ken's have introduced a new and welcome diversity into the market, responding to demand for lighter 'lager' style beers served refrigerated in the continental or American style, as well as different varieties of beer such as wheat and fruit beers.

The 1960s and 70s probably saw the low point for British beer drinkers, as the choice of beers available to them shrunk. Taste was sacrificed in favour of convenience. British beer drinkers over the age of 50 will remember with horror the fizzy, characterless beers of that time, like Double Diamond and Watney's Keg Red Barrel, which were once the only beers on tap in many British pubs. Out of this drought of good beer emerged a campaign – The Campaign for Real Ale (CAMRA) – whose aim was to preserve traditional 'real' beer-making. Forty years later the organisation still thrives, with over 100,000 members and its own annual *Good Beer Guide*, which features pubs serving the UK's most 'interesting' beers.

If you are drinking in a pub you may have your beer, whether a pint or a half-pint, served in the traditional beer glass, like the one shown here. Sometimes called a 'handle' or 'jug', its dimpled sides and sturdy handle make it robust but heavy. It speaks of an age when beer drinkers had a much more limited choice of beer – darker beers like bitter, mild, stout or pale ale – not the lager-type beers increasingly favoured today. You can grip the glass by the handle if you want, but the dimples on the side make it easy to hold by wrapping your hand around it, slipping your fingers inside the handle. The glass is thick so it is durable; and the handle makes it easy to store, hung from a hook over the bar. A genuine (overlooked) everyday icon. ■

Old Thumper,

Hobgoblin,

Fursty Ferret,

Waggle Dance,

Bruins Ruin,

Piddle in the Hole

Eddie Stobart lorry

Eddie Stobart is a transport company that has operated large lorries up and down Britain for over 40 years. It is now so large that it claims its vehicles cover the equivalent of 24 laps of the earth every day and that it makes a delivery in Europe every 20 seconds. A remarkable commercial success, but otherwise you might say: nothing unusual.

What is remarkable about Eddie Stobart is that over that time it has captured the imagination of the British public so strongly that it now has its own fan club, which people pay to join. It sells models of its vehicles, has its own range of cartoon characters and has even inspired a song 'I wanna be an Eddie Stobart Driver'.

Quite how Eddie Stobart came to gain such a unique place in popular British culture is unclear. Perhaps it has something to do with the unusual, but friendly name, which is written in large, clear script on the side of all its vehicles. Perhaps it is also reinforced by the consistent green, red and white colour scheme on its lorries, which from the start 'Steady' Eddie Stobart insisted should be kept smart and clean. Eddie also required his drivers to wear shirts and ties.

Or perhaps Eddie Stobart's popularity is connected to the way the firm gives all its lorries names – mostly female ones, the originals being Twiggy, Dolly, Tammy and Suzi. This has encouraged an army of spotters – presumably bored on long motorway journeys – to record their sightings of the firm's lorries. Members of the fan club can even ask to name a lorry, but in case you are tempted to apply you should note that there is a three-year waiting list. ∎

Eddie Stobart has captured the public imagination

so strongly that it now has its own fan club

Pork pie

The Pork Pie is a traditional English meat pie, made with seasoned chopped pork, sealed in a thin coating of jelly and wrapped in a pastry case. Eat it cold, or if you are lucky, warm, fresh from the oven, on its own, or with brown sauce, pickles or salad.

The best known is the Melton Mowbray Pork Pie, which has recently been granted protected status by the EU. If it says Melton Mowbray on the label then the pie will have been made by one of just ten licensed producers from the region around Melton Mowbray in Leicestershire. It will have been made using fresh, chopped (not minced) pork and will look grey (not as unappetising as it sounds – just the same colour as normal roast pork), not pink like pork pies made from cured pork.

Many people in England take their pork pies very seriously. The Pork Pie Appreciation Society, started in 1982 by some less than dedicated fitness enthusiasts, meets weekly at the Old Bridge Inn at Ripponden in Yorkshire. Each week its members bring along pies, rating them out of ten for taste, texture and general appeal. Its annual Pork Pie competition, held around Easter time, allows the Pork Pie experience to be opened up to others in the area.

And for those further afield the forum on the Society's website caters for any questions members may have about pork pies, such as 'Do we like the jelly in pork pies??' Answer: not if there's too much of it. Or: 'How can an expat living in New Mexico get his hands on a decent pork pie?' Answer: contact the English Pork Pie Company in New York (whose owners used to make pork pies in Yorkshire) and get them to ship some freshly baked ones out by FedEx.

Questions can even extend to those normally dealt with by agony aunts, such as that from a frustrated Pork Pie eater worried about losing his 'hot' girlfriend: 'I love eating a nice Pork Pie but my girlfriend constantly teases me. How can I convince her that they are OK to eat and I won't turn into a marshmallow who takes up 2 seats?' Answer: Limit yourself to one pie a week and take some exercise. ∎

'How can I convince her I won't turn into a marshmallow who takes up two seats?'

Manchester United football shirt

For football-loving children in Manchester – and all over the world, for that matter – there is only one shirt they want to wear: Manchester United. Of course fans of its local rival, Manchester City, will be quick to point out that United is not actually based in Manchester at all. Its ground at Old Trafford is technically in Salford. They may also claim that most of its fans do not even live anywhere near Manchester, but the fact remains that United consistently fills its 76,000 capacity stadium while City struggles to reach 48,000. Somehow Manchester United retains a unique charisma that irks its rival fans. And valued by Forbes at over $2 billion, it is now the most valuable club in the world, selling $150 million worth of merchandise (including shirts) each year. The key to this popularity lies in the club's history.

Things did not start well for the club. Formed by the Lancashire and Yorkshire Railway in 1878 as Newton Heath Football Club it joined the new Football League in its top Division, but after two seasons was relegated to the Second Division. Worse was to come. By 1902 it was on the brink of bankruptcy and had to be rescued by local businessmen. They renamed the club Manchester United. In 1910, not long after winning its first championship title, the club moved to a new stadium at Old Trafford, where it has remained to this day.

The club's fortunes between the two world wars went up and then down, with relegation followed by promotion and relegation once more, but after the Second World War, under legendary manager Matt Busby, the club achieved more consistent success with a team of hand-picked young players, who came to be known as the 'Busby Babes'. But then disaster hit the club once again. Returning from a match in 1958, the team's plane skidded off the runway in snow at Munich Airport, and 23 people including eight star players were killed, with others badly injured.

Through the 1960s Busby rebuilt his team and in 1968 was rewarded when United won the European Cup, the first English team to do so. That team included legendary players such as Bobby Charlton, Dennis Law and George Best. From 1969, when Busby retired, the club went through a number of managers before Sir Alex Ferguson joined in 1986. The club continued to struggle but Ferguson managed to cling on and gradually build its strength, culminating in winning the coveted treble in 1999. That year the club won the Premier League, the FA Cup and the UEFA Champions League, becoming the first English club to achieve this feat.

It is impossible to create that kind of back story overnight. Like Ferrari in motor racing, Manchester United remains appealing precisely because it has had its ups and downs over many years. And that is why small boys all over the world will continue to badger their parents with demands for the latest shirt design, bearing the ever-changing names of its sponsors. ■

Manchester United's ground is not in Manchester

Haggis

Haggis tastes better than you dare to expect. Knowing that it is made of a sheep's heart, liver and lungs minced with onion, oatmeal and suet, and cooked in an animal's intestine for three hours does not at first sound promising. But the reality, however, can be surprisingly good: a sausage or pudding with a nutty texture and a pleasing savoury taste.

Haggis is the traditional Scottish dish, its status confirmed by the country's foremost poet, Robert Burns, in his poem, 'Address to a Haggis' written in 1787.

All over Scotland, and in any part of the world where Scots now live, Burns Night (25 January, the poet's birthday) is the night on which to eat haggis, served with neeps (swede) and tatties (potatoes) washed down with a dram of Scotch whisky. ∎

A nutty texture and a pleasing savoury taste

Christmas cracker

The Christmas Cracker is a vital part of the traditional British Christmas dinner. Family members – children, parents, grandparents, aunts, cousins and friends – pull crackers with one another at the start of the meal and will then be seen, young and old, wearing the coloured paper hats taken from inside them.

The Christmas cracker was invented by a London baker called Thomas J Smith in the 1840s. Sales of his wrapped bon-bon sweets had been disappointing so he decided to make them more appealing by adding mottos inside the twisted paper wrapping, rather in the style of the fortune cookie. But it was only when he added the cracker – a small explosion generated by chemicals on two paper strips, set off by friction – that sales started to grow.

Smith had to make the wrapper bigger to accommodate the cracker mechanism, and in due course the sweet was replaced by a small gift. The paper party hat followed. The gift will vary in quality depending on the price paid for the cracker, but might be anything from a plastic paper clip, a puzzle, a small screwdriver or a key ring to a pair of nail clippers.

Although most people would consider the cracker to be perfectly safe, as it contains only the most minimal amount of explosive material, British law takes a more alarmist view. It classifies crackers as fireworks. This means they cannot be legally sold to anyone under 16. Not only that but they are typically accompanied by a stern warning on the box telling users to 'pull crackers away from the face and at arm's length' and not to pull the snap outside the cracker.

An important element in the contemporary cracker is the inclusion of a joke (or sometimes a motto or riddle) and the joke is invariably very bad. Examples:

Question: What do you call a blind reindeer?
Answer: No eye deer.

Question: What's furry and minty?
Answer: A polo bear.

Question: What do you call a penguin in the Sahara desert?
Answer: Lost.

Some claim that the jokes are deliberately terrible so that this puts less pressure on the person reading it out. After all, if the joke is known to be weak then no one can blame the teller for failing to do it justice. Whatever the truth, it is hard to imagine a British family Christmas that does not include the traditional Christmas cracker, even if it does only contain a cheap paper hat, a useless gift and a weak joke. ■

Question: What do you call a penguin in the Sahara desert? Answer: Lost

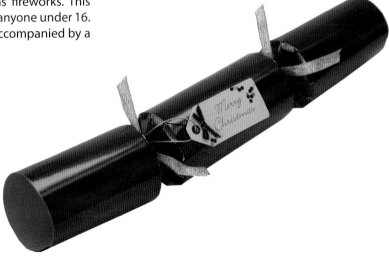

Remembrance poppy

The Remembrance poppy consists of a green plastic stem with a single green paper leaf, a red petal cluster and a black centre. It appears each year as part of the Royal British Legion's Poppy Appeal. In this simple form the Poppy is unpretentious. It is after all not the object, but the sentiment behind it that counts. You can, if you want, buy more expensive poppies: for example a poppy brooch encrusted with Swarovski crystals was auctioned in 2007 for almost £2,850, but such poppies are unusual.

The Remembrance poppy appears in autumn every year, usually sold from small counter-top display units in shops, clubs and pubs, or in the street by volunteers. Poppies are worn on Remembrance Day, the Sunday nearest to 11 November each year, which honours those who gave their lives fighting in wars, in particular, World War One. The money raised – nearly £40 million each year – is used to improve the lives of the war survivors, many of whom have to cope with severe injuries.

Why Red Poppies? Apart from the obvious significance of red as a symbol of blood shed by soldiers, they are mentioned in the famous poem 'In Flanders fields', written during World War One a Canadian officer called John McRae, who was inspired by the resilience of the red poppies that continued to grow – against all odds – in the battlefields of Belgium:

> In Flanders fields the poppies blow
> Between the crosses, row on row. ■

A poppy brooch encrusted with Swarovski crystals was auctioned in 2007 for £2,850

School uniform

The earliest records of school uniforms in Britain date back to the 16th century. So-called Bluecoat schools required their schoolboys and apprentices to wear long blue coats – blue being favoured because it was a cheap dye, and so was affordable, as well as suggesting humility. Christ's Hospital School in Sussex retains a form of this coat as part of its uniform to this day.

The uniform shown here is that worn by students at Stockport Grammar School, whose history dates back to 1487, when it was founded by Sir Edmond Shaa – Mayor of London. Most schools in Britain, including those with much shorter history, require a uniform, usually consisting of at least a blazer or sweater in school colours, together with a dark skirt or trousers.

For centuries education in Britain was the preserve of the rich or of the beneficiaries of charity, attending schools which were often controlled by the Church. It was not until 1870 that the Elementary Education Act introduced free primary education for all children up to the age of 12 and most of the new schools founded at that time required a uniform.

Whilst the origins of many school uniforms date back a long time, the wearing of them still provokes debate. Those in favour argue that a uniform is a leveller, preventing children with richer parents from showing off in the latest designer wear, and that it promotes a sense of belonging. They also suggest that school uniform can also provide schoolchildren with a relatively harmless focus for their teenage rebellion as they look for creative ways to bend the rules. Opponents of uniforms on the other hand argue that they are old-fashioned and an unnecessary expense; that staff end up spending too much time policing the rules and that uniforms stifle individuality.

Many schools have now acted to simplify or modernise their uniforms, for example, by allowing boys to dispense with ties and blazers and letting girls wear trousers. For the moment, though, there is no sign of any move to change national policy on school uniforms, as all the major political parties are still in favour of them. ▪

A harmless focus for rebellion, or old-fashioned and unnecessary?

Red double-decker bus

What do a Ferrari and a double-decker bus have in common? The answer (apart from the obvious one that they both have an engine and wheels) is that they look best in a bright scarlet red. Double-deckers exist all over the world, but the red double-decker bus is instantly associated with Britain in general, and with London in particular.

When London Bridge was dismantled and moved to Lake Havasu City in Arizona in 1967, the buyer Robert P. McCulloch also purchased some red double-decker buses to add authenticity to the English themed shopping mall that he built alongside it. When London took over the Olympic baton from Beijing in 2008 the Mayor of London, Boris Johnson, together with David Beckham and other British celebrities, drove into the

Bird's Nest stadium on the top of an open-topped red double decker. The travel writer Jan Morris once wrote of her delight on returning to London from a trip and being struck by the sheer redness of the London buses.

The red London bus even inspired its own song, written and performed by the duo Flanders & Swann. Titled 'A Transport of Delight' it sang the praises of 'That big six-wheeler,

scarlet-painted, London Transport, diesel-engined, ninety-seven horse-power omnibus!'

The best known London bus is the Routemaster, introduced in 1956, which saw active service in London for almost 50 years (and you will still see some of them on the streets of London today). Many of these buses covered millions of miles and were then refurbished and sold abroad. When they were phased out from general use in 2005 there was some outcry because they were replaced by the longer and more cumbersome bendy bus.

Now they are being replaced by a 21st century Routemaster, called, rather less elegantly, the New Bus for London, and shown here. Designed by Thomas Heatherwick Studios and built by Wrightbus in Ballymeena in Northern Ireland, the new bus includes the same hop-on, hop-off platform as the original, but naturally uses new more energy efficient technology. ■

What do a Ferrari and a double-decker bus have in common?

Wellington boots

The Wellington boot, often known as a 'welly' or gumboot, was originally made of leather and popularised by a famous British military leader, Arthur Wellesley, the first Duke of Wellington. Later known as the Iron Duke, Wellington became a British hero after he defeated the French leader Napoleon at the Battle of Waterloo in 1815.

Wellington wanted a boot which would be hard wearing for battle, yet comfortable if worn in the evening, and he instructed his shoemaker, Hoby of St James's Street in London, to create a long tight-fitting boot which would meet his requirements.

Wellington boots quickly caught on with patriotic British gentlemen eager to copy their war hero. You could say that the Wellington boot was then a little like the four-wheel drive SUV today. It suggested the ability to cope with the toughest conditions, even though most of the time he (and his boots) never ventured beyond the comfortable surroundings of London.

The best-known British brand of wellington boot is Hunter, which was started in the late 19th century when an American gentleman called Mr Henry Lee Norris moved from the United States to Scotland and set up a new factory making wellington boots not from leather, but from rubber.

After seeing service in two World Wars, Hunter boots became increasingly popular with the general public, especially with gardeners, walkers and farm workers. In 1955 Hunter introduced the green welly, which came to be identified with a particular kind of person who would spend the weekends in the country and the week in the city. Such people quickly became known as the 'green welly brigade'.

In 1976, having supplied wellingtons to the Royal Households, Hunter was awarded a Royal Warrant. Since then Hunter boots have become an essential fashion item which is more often associated with music festivals like Glastonbury than any more hazardous pursuit. Alex James from the Brit band Blur recommended that all festival-goers should equip themselves with the five W's: wet wipes, wallet, wigwam (tent), waterproof coat and of course wellingtons.

Over the centuries Britain has introduced a number of new sports to the world, from football to rugby and cricket. Not least of these is the sport of 'welly wanging' or welly throwing – which originated in Britain at a place called Upperthong near Holmfirth in Yorkshire. Each year the World Welly Wanging Championship is held at Upperthong as part of its Gala, held around the end of June. ▥

Britain has introduced a number of new sports to the world... not least of which is the sport of welly wanging

Irn-Bru

Irn-Bru is a fizzy non-alcoholic drink produced in Scotland, and its unusual name and quirky advertising over many years has given it a distinctively Scottish character. You can buy it throughout the United Kingdom, and elsewhere in the world, for that matter – anywhere where there is a large community of people from its native Scotland. Irn-Bru is so popular in Scotland that it outsells global brands such as Coca-Cola and Pepsi. Known for its bright orange colour and sweet, slightly citrus flavour, the Irn-Bru recipe, like that of Coca Cola, is a closely guarded secret.

Originally called 'Iron Brew', it is thought that the name originated when Glasgow Central Station was being rebuilt in 1901. To discourage workers from the William Beardmore and Company Steel Works in Glasgow from quenching their thirst with large quantities of beer (and so becoming incapable of working properly) a non-alcoholic source of refreshment was sought. Local drinks manufacturer, A. G. Barr, offered a soft drink and the name arose because of its connections to the steel and iron works. Far from being alcoholic, some claim that Irn-Bru is actually a highly effective hangover cure.

In 1946 a change in the law required A. G. Barr to update the name as the drink is not actually brewed. That was when the phonetic spelling was substituted, Irn-Bru, mimicking the pronunciation in a Glasgow accent.

Advertising of Irn-Bru has always made a point of its Scottishness, referring to it as 'Scotland's other national drink' (after Scotch whisky) or describing it as 'made in Scotland from girders'. One advertising campaign summed up Irn-Bru's appeal more directly: 'If it's not Scottish... It's Crrrap!!!'

When the National Museum of Scotland held an exhibition celebrating the Scottish nation it invited celebrities to select appropriate exhibits. Sean Connery chose a crate of Irn-Bru.

Ads for Irn-Bru have also sometimes been controversial, drawing complaints from the public. For example one campaign featured a young woman in a bikini, accompanied by the slogan 'I never knew four and a half inches could give so much pleasure'. Another depicted a cow saying: 'When I'm a burger, I want to be washed down with Irn-Bru', while yet another had a black and white picture of a well-dressed but stuffy-looking older man saying 'I don't like Irn-Bru but I'm just a silly old banker'. As far as we know there were no complaints about this ad. ■

Scotland's other national drink

Dr Martens boots

The first Dr Martens boot made by the Griggs family at their Rushden factory in Northamptonshire in 1960 was almost identical to the one shown here. And the boot is still in production today, still made by hand at the original factory using the same construction methods and still using the company's '59' last. The upper and sole are still sewn together using the distinctive yellow thread known to generations of customers of Dr Martens – better known as Doc Martens or DMs.

The original concept behind Doc Martens was to create a working boot using an air-cushioned sole to aid comfort. Credit for the design goes to the original Doctor Märtens, a German who invented them when he hurt his ankle in a skiing accident. The British company Griggs, who took up the license to make them was at first glance an unlikely licensee, being a traditional British shoe manufacturer, more associated with hand-made shoes for the gentry. But the boot, marketed under the brand name Airwair,

achieved rapid success in a new market that Griggs had not attracted up to then – the working class. It was popular with working people who were on their feet a lot – people like postmen, construction workers, factory workers and policemen.

Then something happened that transformed the public perception of this serious, practical and above all functional boot. It was adopted by the youth generation.

In 1966 the guitar-destroying rocker Pete Townshend started wearing Doc Martens on stage when performing with The Who. He liked the air-cushioned sole (which helped him leap around on stage) and he liked the way they reminded him of his working class upbringing. Doc Martens started to become cool.

What is most remarkable about Doc Martens is that they have continued to be cool ever since, being constantly worn by new generations of fashionable people. Part of the appeal is that Doc Martens are tough and carry an aura of danger.

In the 1970s they were adopted by skinheads, some of whom would expose the steel toecaps of their boots to make them more intimidating, later they were taken up by punks. And all the while they continued to be popular with policeman, many of whom would be confronting protestors and angry young men, all of them wearing Doc Martens. How many other products appeal so powerfully to both law makers and law breakers, to free-thinkers and to the establishment?

For a while after 2003 production of Doc Martens stopped in Britain and was moved to China and Thailand but in 2007 it came back. In 2010 a Doc Martens boot won two fashion awards at the 2010 Fashion Show in New York City; one for the 'most popular men's footwear in latest fashion' and the other for 'best counter-cultural footwear of the decade'.

You can now buy the Doc Martens 1460 boot in green, purple, pink or a range of other colours. You can even buy it with an old-style flower design – called Victorian flowers. Not the recommended choice if you want to look tough. ■

How many other products appeal so powerfully to both law makers and law breakers, to free-thinkers and to the establishment?

Bottle of Scotch whisky

Whisky has been produced in Scotland for centuries, possibly for a thousand years (the earliest written record goes back to the 15th century). A word of warning here: Scotch whisky should not be confused with whiskey with an 'e', which typically refers to Irish or North American alternatives. To indicate just how significant a part whisky plays in Scottish culture, the word whisky itself comes from the Gaelic *usquebaugh*, which means 'water of life'.

If you really want to get to grips with Scotch whisky then you should go on a Scotch whisky tour, which will take you on a round of tastings at distilleries all over Scotland, the limits set only by your stamina and your ability to stay sober.

Alternatively, if you want to appreciate Scotch whisky better but without the travel, you could order a 'Scotch whisky aroma nosing kit' which will give you up to 24 samples of Scotch whisky 'aromas' covering the spectrum typically found in Scotch whiskies, together with a guide book. By this means you will be able to impress your friends by talking convincingly about the best 'nosing action' and overwhelm them with your knowledge of the little-known hazard of 'tired nose syndrome'.

Most of the Scotch whisky that you will find both in Scotland and in bars around the world is blended – in other words it has been created by combining whiskies produced by a number of different distilleries. Typical brands are Bells, Dewar's and Johnnie Walker.

For real Scotch whisky afficionados, unfortunately there is nothing to compare with a fine single malt whisky, such as the 21-year-old single malt pictured here, from Old Pulteney in Wick – made using malted barley at a single distillery and then matured for at least three years in oak casks previously used for bourbon or sherry. The finest of these Scotches have been matured for 40 years or more and are, not surprisingly, very expensive. ∎

You will be able to impress your friends by talking convincingly about the best 'Nosing Action' and 'Tired Nose Syndrome'

Dyson vacuum cleaner

The Dyson vacuum cleaner looks just as futuristic now as it did when it first smashed its way into the uninspiring world of vacuum cleaners in the 1980s. Like some domestic 'Transformer' with its mechanical intestines exposed, it combined striking looks with a revolutionary cyclone technology, which delivered higher performance than the average vacuum cleaner. It broke new ground too by featuring a clear plastic bin which not only allowed the user the satisfaction of seeing how much dust they had collected, but also did away with the hated dust bag.

The vacuum cleaner first became common in British homes around the 1960s and the leading brand at that time was Hoover. So widespread was its use that many British people still use the word Hoover to describe any vacuum cleaner, regardless of the actual brand. Today however it is Dyson, rather than Hoover, that sells the greatest number of vacuum cleaners in the UK.

If James Dyson were American he would probably be admired as the embodiment of the American dream: a man who passionately believed in making things better, who got into debt in pursuit of his dream and who, most importantly of all, succeeded in his quest and became one of the richest men in the country. He would be the Steve Jobs (or, from another age, the Thomas Edison) of domestic appliances. But the British do things in a rather understated way, so although James Dyson is widely admired and his products are bought in large numbers, he remains mostly out of the mainstream media spotlight.

Dyson's first successful product was a wheelbarrow which used a plastic ball instead of a wheel, which he called the Ballbarrow. But it was when in the 1970s he turned his attention to the vacuum cleaner that he really hit the jackpot. Noticing that traditional vacuum cleaners, which use bags to catch the dust lost efficiency very quickly, he set about developing a new kind of cleaner, using the cyclonic separation principle, that would do away with bags altogether.

When other manufacturers turned him away Dyson was undeterred and set up his own manufacturing company. He claims it took him 'fifteen years of frustration, perseverance, and over 5,000 prototypes' to launch the Dyson DC01 vacuum cleaner under his own name. Within 22 months it became the best-selling cleaner in the UK. 'I wanted to give up almost every day... A lot of people give up when the world seems to be against them, but that's the point when you should push a little harder.'

Seeing his success, other makers, including Hoover, have had to introduce their own cyclone cleaners. In a sad footnote to its one-time domination of the vacuum cleaner market, Hoover not only saw its market share crumble but was also found guilty of infringing one of James Dyson's patents, having to pay him a reputed $5 million in damages. ∎

Within 22 months it became the best-selling cleaner in the UK

AGA cooker

It was Nobel-prize-winning Swedish physicist Gustaf Dalén who invented the heat storage cooker in 1922. At the time he was working for a Swedish company, AGA, and had been blinded by an explosion at work. While recuperating at home Dalén came up with the idea for a new kind of cooker, which would save his wife the need to keep relighting her solid fuel stove.

Dalén did not however win his Nobel Prize for inventing the AGA. Instead that was awarded for his pioneering work in developing automated lighthouses. The AGA company in Sweden continues to this day but no longer makes heat storage cookers or lighthouses. (It is now best known as a producer of industrial gases.)

Meanwhile, in Britain, there is another company independent from the Swedish AGA, called AGA Rangemaster. The latter took out a licence from the Swedish company in 1929, and has carried on making the world-famous AGA, and later also Rayburn heat storage cookers, ever since.

Invented by a blind physicist who won a Nobel prize for developing automated lighthouses

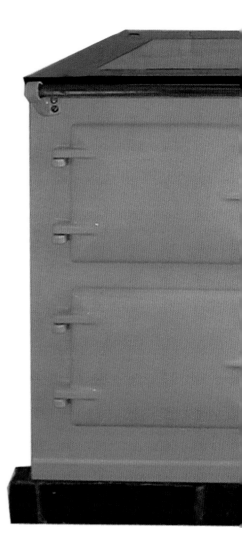

The AGA is the cooker of choice for well-off British people with larger than average houses. Too big to fit in the average British kitchen, the AGA is also quite a bit too expensive for most people's budgets, costing as much as £10,000 or more, whereas a regular cooker can be bought for well under £1000.

Because the AGA is on all the time and remains constantly hot there is no need to keep switching it on and off, making it convenient to use, and it keeps the kitchen snug and welcoming in a chilly British winter.

This of course can become a drawback in summer, and the company has recently developed electric versions that can be switched on and off, conserving energy.

The AGA is most at home in the generously sized kitchen of a large Victorian house, a converted barn or country farmhouse. It has also become associated with a certain kind of novel, known as the 'AGA saga', written in the 1990s by the novelist Joanna Trollope and which typically featured well-off middle-class women living in country villages in the south of England. ▪

Cornish pasty

The Cornish pasty is a protected species, just like the Great Crested Newt and the Fisher's Estuarine Moth. Not that it was in any danger of disappearing like the newt or the moth; rather the opposite. It was under threat because the genuine Cornish-made pasty was being swamped by other species, all made elsewhere, but pretending to be the real thing.

Since 2011 the Cornish pasty has gained Protected Geographical Indication (PGI) status under EU law. This means that a genuine Cornish pasty now has to be made in Cornwall, it must have the distinctive 'D' shaped pastry case – crimped at the side rather than at the top – and it must contain chunks of beef, potato, swede (but never carrot) and onion. Seasoning is added, but no artificial flavourings or preservatives and then it is baked slowly.

You will find pasties in other parts of the world, but almost always because they were taken there by emigrating Cornishmen. For hundreds of years Cornish working people had eaten pasties; it became the traditional Cornishman's packed lunch, easy to make and easy to eat whether out on Bodmin Moor or down a tin mine, and today it offers the same advantages.

Some have suggested that Cornish pasties were side-crimped so that miners could eat holding them by their thick edge. They would then throw the crust away after eating the rest, so avoiding contact between dirty fingers and food. This seems unlikely, however, given that the miners were not well off and would scarcely have thrown away good food. In addition there are photos showing people eating pasties wrapped in paper or muslin; a much simpler and less wasteful solution.

'Oggy' is a slang term for a Cornish pasty, derived from its Cornish name, 'hoggan'. Legend has it that tin-miners' wives or pasty bakers would shout 'oggy oggy oggy' to announce that pasties were ready, with the miners responding 'oi! oi! oi!' in acknowledgment. More recently, this has been adopted as a popular rugby chant.

You will find Cornish pasties on sale at London's busy Euston Station serving rushed commuters, but really, a pasty should be eaten sitting on a sea wall or a rock in Looe or Padstow, with the sound of gulls in the background. ■

A protected species like the Great Crested Newt and Fisher's Estuarine Moth

Welsh laverbread

Laver is an edible seaweed that grows along the coastline of the Irish Sea, around the western shores of Britain and down the east side of Ireland. It is used for making laverbread – a traditional Welsh delicacy, known locally there as Bara Lawr and referred to by some as 'Welshman's Caviar'.

Although the laver grows plentifully along the Irish sea coast it is laborious to pick and there is no way of automating the process, so it has to be gathered by hand. Once picked the laver must be rinsed thoroughly, before boiling and then mincing, to create a paste-like texture. And this process gives it another similarity to caviar – it tends to be expensive, costing £14 or more (including delivery) for 200 g if bought online.

At first sight, when you open a pack of laverbread it can be a little off-putting, as you are faced with a dark, slightly sinister looking, slimy gunge. But do not be put off. If you are used to eating say cooked spinach and you like seafood, then laverbread should hold no fears. A quick taste of the raw paste reveals a sea-salty flavour tinged with the same iron tang that you get with cooked spinach or spring greens. And laverbread is highly nutritious, rich in protein along with important minerals iron and iodine, and containing vitamins A, B, B2, C and D. It is also very low in calories.

Whilst laverbread is of course vegetarian, many recipes combine it with bacon or seafood. Probably the simplest and most common is the Welsh Breakfast cake, which is made by coating laverbread in oatmeal, frying it and serving with freshly cooked bacon, but it can also be served with cockles, smoked mussels or even oysters. ■

'Welshman's caviar'

Tesco carrier bag

In Hollywood movies the hero or heroine emerging from their local grocery store will typically be clutching a brown paper bag stuffed with their purchases. In Britain it would be a plastic bag branded with the name of one of the country's leading supermarkets – Tesco, Sainsbury's, Waitrose, ASDA or Morrisons. We get through more than 12 billion plastic bags each year and 2 million of those will bear the red and blue Tesco logo. Such is Tesco's leadership in the British high street that it now accounts for one pound in every eight spent by British consumers, and not surprisingly it gets through more bags than its competitors too.

But that's all changing. Consumers are being encouraged to buy and use reusable bags, to reduce plastic consumption, waste and pollution. And it seems to be working. Tesco reports a 50 per cent drop in demand for its free plastic carrier bags, whose numbers may in any case be threatened by legislation.

Since October 2011 Welsh retailers have been obliged by law to charge five pence for each carrier bag used by customers. We can be pretty sure that the other member countries of the UK will be watching how that particular initiative goes. ■

We get through 12 billion plastic bags each year

Hunting pink

Hunting pink is the term used to describe the traditional clothing worn by those who hunt in Britain. And you may well wonder why it is called 'pink' when it is so obviously bright red. The usual explanation is that it was named after one Thomas Pink, a tailor who made hunting jackets. But it seems that the hunting outfit was already being called pink some time before Pink the tailor came on the scene.

Another suggestion is that in the past pink was often used to mean 'excellent', (just as today someone might say they are 'in the pink', meaning that they feel very well), but again there is no obvious link to hunting.

Today the British seem to be in two minds about hunting. On the one hand, Christmas cards often carry scenes of rural Britain with hunters in red riding across snow-covered fields and hounds in pursuit of a fleeing fox. At Christmas time people love this warm, nostalgic view of an idyllic rural past, but there has also been a long tradition of hunt protesters objecting to what they see as the cruelty of fox hunting. Their campaigns to disrupt hunts by laying false trails or getting in the way of the horses led to new legislation being passed in 2004. Since 2005 hunting has been illegal throughout the country under an Act of Parliament passed by the Labour government.

Hunts do continue to take place as The Hunting Act 2004 only stops hunting where an animal is being chased; it does not stop 'drag hunting' – where dogs are trained to follow an artificial scent. Traditionally hunting has always been viewed as an upper class pastime, and though there is some evidence that its appeal is now widening, it still remains very much a minority sport.

For now hunting remains an activity loved by a few, violently opposed by others and largely ignored by the majority. There is no doubt though that many hunt groups do still feel under threat and are looking to lower their profile. This could, in turn, threaten the hunting pink, as some hunts are now moving away from the eye-catching red costume in favour of less conspicuous tweeds, known as 'ratcatchers'.

No doubt this helps them blend into the countryside better than the bright red hunting pink, but an old British tradition is being lost, much like the disappearing red telephone box. ■

Some hunts are moving away from the traditional red costume in favour of 'ratcatchers'

Garden shed

A shed is usually a simple, single-storey structure in a back garden or on an allotment which is generally used for storage, for hobbies or as a workshop. Of course sheds exist all over the world, but in Britain the shed has particular cultural significance. It is where British people, especially men, retreat to, in order to 'potter', to escape, to 'do stuff'.

It is their refuge from the rest of the world, a place where where they can dismantle a motorbike without having to suffer the abuse they might otherwise earn if they carried out the same task on the kitchen table. In exceptional circumstances the shed may also be used to sleep in if their owners have locked themselves out after a night at the pub. And whilst it may still be men who most often seek refuge in their shed, increasingly women are also enjoying their own space there.

The typical British garden shed is small – as little as three or four square metres of floor space – and made of wood, usually with at least one window. Gardeners use theirs as a potting shed, whilst hobbyists pursue their favoured leisure interests, which could include activities such as wood-turning, pottery, painting, or laying out model railways.

Many owners take their sheds very seriously. If you look on the website www.readersshed.co.uk you will find examples of sheds designed to resemble Roman temples; sheds that look like the Tardis (the police box time machine used by Doctor Who in the long-running BBC television series); several pubs-in-sheds, as well as eco-sheds made of straw bales or rammed earth. Each year paint manufacturer Cuprinol sponsors a Shed of the Year competition and any of the 15 million shed owners in the UK is welcome to enter.

Famous writers like Daphne Du Maurier, Philip Pullman and Roald Dahl all used their sheds to write in. Roald Dahl's shed was so grand that his surviving family even launched an appeal for £500,000 to restore it (though the public reaction to this was lukewarm at best, as few could see how any shed could cost the equivalent of a good-sized house).

Probably the most appealing association of the garden shed, though, is with inventors, working on a minimal budget, who come up with ideas – some wonderful, some ridiculous, but always fascinating. In 2011 the energy company Powergen even launched a competition for garden shed inventors with new ideas for green products to compete for a £50,000 prize. On the panel is serial inventor Trevor Baylis, who himself came up with the wind-up radio and the mobile-phone-charging shoe in his own garden shed. ■

In exceptional circumstances the shed may also be used to sleep in if their owners have locked themselves out after a night at the pub

Three-pin plug

It seems as though every nation has to establish its own identity by having its own unique design of electrical plug and socket: two flat pins in the USA, two round ones in continental Europe, and in Britain? Three square pins.

The standard British plug is distinctive but not very elegant. With its large body and long squared-off pins, it looks like a dead, overweight three-legged beetle.

The original design was created 70 years ago, and until recently no effort has been put into revising it, probably because no one saw any pressing need to do so. Concerned that the previous two-pin system could be dangerous, a government-appointed committee came up with this solution just after World War Two. The third pin that they specified is a safety earth which prevents access to the live connections, for example if a small child tries to push its fingers into the socket.

Over the years, when most appliances were simply plugged into the wall and stayed there until they were replaced, there was little pressure to change the design of the three-pin plug. Now, however, we use a greater number of portable electrical devices that we plug in and then carry around, the most obvious being the laptop computer. The bulk of the three-pin plug has therefore become a real problem.

Seeing this new requirement, Min-Kyu Choi, a graduate of the Royal College of Art, has designed a collapsible version that reduces the thickness of the plug to that of an Apple MacBook Air, the thinnest laptop currently on the market. By allowing the two live pins to turn though 90 degrees he has created a plug that will fit into existing wall sockets, but which can also quickly and effectively be folded away flat for storage in a laptop bag. ∎

Like a dead, overweight three-legged beetle

Yorkshire pudding

The Yorkshire pudding is a key ingredient in the traditional British Sunday dinner, which consists of roasted meat, roast potatoes, with vegetables and gravy and... Yorkshire pudding. The meat is normally beef, a meat so much part of British history that the French at one time called British people 'Les Rosbifs' (The Roast Beefs) – one of the more complimentary things that the French have thought to call their neighbours over the centuries. Yorkshire pudding is not just served with beef, though; it can also accompany other meats such as pork, lamb, or chicken, or vegetarian options such as nut roast.

The Yorkshire pudding is made with milk, flour and eggs – similar to the mixture used to make pancakes – which rises during cooking. It can either be made as a single large dish, which is then cut up before serving, or as smaller individual puddings like the one pictured here.

No one is entirely sure how or why the Yorkshire pudding originally came about. It could have been chosen as a way of using up the fat that would drip from meat when it was cooked, but perhaps more importantly in poorer households it would be served as a separate dish, before the more expensive meat dish, intended as a way of reducing the appetite. A variant of the Yorkshire pudding is toad-in-the-hole, which is a Yorkshire pudding with sausages baked into it – served as a dish in its own right. ■

The French at one time called British people 'Les Rosbifs'

Teapot

If you had asked a visitor to Britain 70 years ago to list the things that seemed to them most typically, and eccentrically, British, they might well have counted off things like the complicated money system with its pounds, shillings and pence. Others might have mentioned the warm beer, or the random Imperial weights and measures system with its stones, pounds and ounces. But the one thing no one could not possibly have failed to mention would have been the cultural importance to the British people of tea.

At that time tea was always brewed in a pot and served formally at afternoon tea by your hostess, pouring from a beautifully decorated china pot kept warm by a tea cosy. It would be contrary to etiquette for anyone else to take control of the teapot, and a common phrase at the time, if there was no hostess present, was 'Shall I be mother?'.

Since that time Britons have discovered the pleasures of well-made coffee, but tea remains the archetypal British hot drink, whether it is the usual English Breakfast tea or other varieties which have become increasingly popular such as Earl Grey and green tea, or caffeine free options like rooibos, fruit teas and herbal teas.

'Shall I be mother?'

British society started to become less formal from the 1960s on, and the formality of making tea in a pot has been replaced by adoption of an American invention: the tea bag. Today more than 90 per cent of tea sold in Britain is in that form and most tea is now made in a cup or mug, without the need for the teapot.

In spite of the decline in teapot usage many contemporary designers continue to play with teapot design and decoration. Designers like Cath Kidston, who makes teapots in distinctive pastel colours, and Emma Bridgewater, whose polka dot teapot is shown here, continue to develop teapot designs in keeping with current customer tastes.

Then there is a wholly different category of teapot owner: the collector. For such people it is not the function but the form of the teapot that counts, and the more extraordinary the better.

The Tea Pottery in Yorkshire caters for just this market, continuing a '200 year old tradition of making eccentric, novelty teapots in fine English ceramics'. Each teapot is cast and decorated by hand and the company specialises in creating teapots in the form of pretty much anything you care to ask for: a caravan, a cake, a cocktail bar, a tent, a wash basin, an espresso machine, a piano (as shown here), or even a replica of the front door of Number 10 Downing Street. ■

Digestive biscuit

The British are by far the biggest biscuit eaters in the world. Their consumption of biscuits, at 8.5 kg per person per year, beats even the USA, who can manage only a pitifully modest 6.3 kg. And at the top of the British biscuit tree sits the Digestive biscuit: hard, crisp, crumbly and (with a little bit of skill) good for dunking in your cup of tea. And there of course lies the secret of the biscuit. It is the perfect match for the British tea break.

The word biscuit refers to the original way they were made – meaning 'twice cooked' in French – and means the same as the American 'cookie'. (Just to be confusing, what the Americans call a biscuit is what the British call a scone, roughly speaking.) Some claim that the term 'digestive' is derived from the belief that these biscuits had antacid properties, due to the use of sodium bicarbonate when they were first developed in the late 19th century. However there are references to digestive biscuits in earlier recipe books, such as the one in *The Royal English and Foreign Confectioner* (1862) which contained just brown flour, salt, a little butter and water. It is unlikely that this recipe would ever have become Britain's favourite biscuit, unlike the current digestive, which is a development of recipes created by Huntley & Palmer and McVitie's.

Digestive biscuits are popular in food preparation for making

The Americans had Watergate. The British had 'Biscuitgate'

into bases for cheesecakes and banoffee pie. Chocolate digestive biscuits, coated on one side with milk, dark or white chocolate, were originally produced by McVitie's in 1925 as the Chocolate Homewheat Digestive. American travel writer Bill Bryson has described the chocolate digestive as a 'British masterpiece'.

Where the Americans had Watergate, the British equivalent was 'Biscuitgate' – a scandal about the British Prime Minister's favourite biscuit. The subject of this world-shattering controversy was the British Prime Minister in 2009, Gordon Brown. The British press accused Brown of being so indecisive that he could not even tell a questioner which was his favourite biscuit. It was alleged that Brown refused to be pinned down in spite of being asked 12 times.

It was later revealed that the question was never put to him at all, and the whole controversy was a press invention. Number 10 Downing Street later confirmed that Brown was especially fond of chocolate biscuits, but by then the story had joined the ranks of popular urban myths, further strengthening the public image of the Prime Minister as a ditherer. He was voted out of office at the election less than a year later – which just goes to show how much biscuits matter to the British people. ∎

Ordnance Survey map

The Ordnance Survey map – with its distinctive contour lines showing height above sea level – has played a major part in encouraging one of the great British pastimes: walking.

The largest organisation for walkers in the UK – Ramblers – boasts just 120,000 members, roughly equivalent to 0.2 per cent of the population, while we have over 30 million cars, one for every two people in the country. But there will be few households in the UK that do not own at least one Ordnance Survey map. Even though digital mapping now accounts for 90 per cent of the Ordnance Survey's business, it still sells more than two million paper maps every year.

The Ordnance Survey map has survived the invention of the satnav because many love its facility not just to plan a route, but also to catch other features of interest along the way. Where many satnavs have left lorries stranded on narrow tracks, too tight for them to pass, no Ordnance Survey map ever so badly misled its user.

The first moves to carry out comprehensive and accurate mapping of Britain date back to early in the 18th century, but it was only in 1791 that fears of an invasion by the French provided the motivation to get systematic mapping work underway.

At that time the Ministry of Defence was known as the Board of Ordnance, which is where the unusual name for the maps has come from. Naturally, as the threat from the French was focused on the south east of England, that was the first area to be mapped. As it happened, the French never did invade, but by then the advantages of mapping the country had been recognised. Over the following years the whole of the United Kingdom was surveyed and recorded.

No longer linked to the military, Ordnance Survey remains a government-owned organisation, having somehow survived the privatisation programmes of the 1980s and 90s that took other similar bodies into private ownership. It pays its own way and has embraced the digital age, for example allowing people to generate their own digital maps, centred on any point they choose.

OS maps are not just for the car, or even for walking or cycling. They are for looking at, for enjoying. Each is a highly resolved work of art, craft, design and cartography. A single map can keep you engrossed for hours on a rainy day, as you discover features of the landscape or intriguing roads and paths that bring out the explorer in you. They are, in short, masterpieces of clear, functional and remarkably beautiful design. ∎

More than 2 million paper maps a year

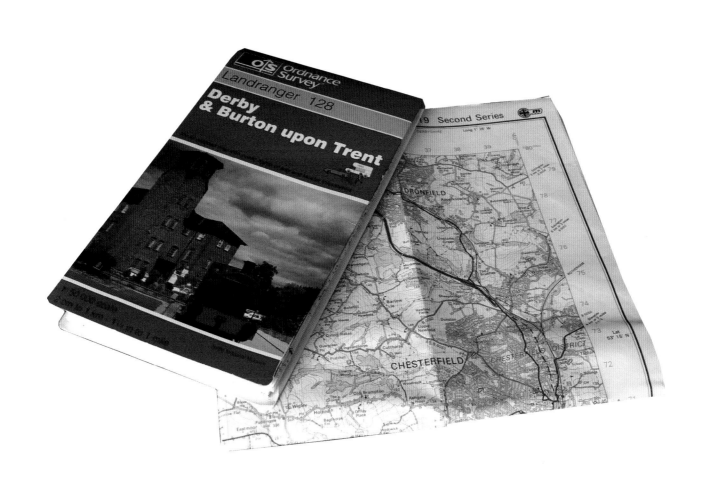

Floral wallpaper

The British have a bit of a love affair with flowers on wallpaper – and on fabrics as well come to that. In 1996 IKEA ran an advertising campaign encouraging British consumers to get rid of all their old floral-patterned furniture, telling them to 'chuck out the chintz!' They were encouraged to embrace IKEA's own simpler Scandinavian aesthetic instead. The campaign was a very successful one and IKEA has been just as successful in the UK as it has been around the world.

Yet so strong is the British love of flowers and floral designs that they have never been persuaded to abandon them completely. In the 1970s Laura Ashley built her empire on fresh floral designs – for dresses, furnishings and wall coverings. Over the last decade, Cath Kidston has added her own distinctive blue and pink pastel floral designs – on houseware, fabrics and wallpapers – to the world of interior decor.

But the granddaddy of them all is probably Sanderson, which can trace its history back to 1860 when Arthur Sanderson started importing French wallpapers. The firm went on over the next 150 years to commission major artists and designers like Pablo Picasso, John Piper and Lucienne Day to create their designs. In the 1970s the company promoted a co-ordinated approach to interior décor by creating floral designs that enabled householders to use the same fabric for wallcoverings, curtains and soft furnishings accompanied by the strapline 'Very Sanderson'.

In its most extreme interpretations it was possible to create a completely camouflaged room in which it was hard to see where the furniture, walls, floors, curtains and people began and ended. The ultimate nightmare for the minimalist.

The greatest of all the exponents of floral wallpaper design was the 19th century designer William Morris, who was also a philosopher, scholar and writer. As the founder of the Arts and Crafts movement Morris created a distinctive 'look' featuring intricate flowing patterns of interwined stems, leaves and flowers, which influenced many designers who followed him. His work is continued today by the company Morris & Co., whose designs can be found on wallpapers, furnishings, bags and even umbrellas. ▪

It was possible to create a completely camouflaged room in which it was hard to see where the furniture, walls, floors, curtains and people began and ended

Tweed jacket

The tweed jacket can be very versatile. As part of a beautifully tailored three piece Savile Row woollen suit, tweed is the epitome of Britishness, or at least of a certain kind of Britishness. An old saying from New York's Madison Avenue ran: 'Think Yiddish, Dress British'. You can still buy your own bespoke Savile Row tweed suit today, from companies that can trace their history back to Victorian times, provided of course that you have $5,000 or so to spend on it.

Originally created as military and riding wear, tweed is hard wearing, sometimes a little rough to the touch, but always aristocratically elegant. With a lighter weight cloth and some design flair it can also be stylish, and at home on the catwalks, bearing designer labels like Westwood and Galliano. At the opposite end of the fashion scale, tweed becomes an old jacket in traditionally earthy shades of brown and green, perhaps with leather elbow patches – the wear of choice for your favourite old schoolteacher.

The original name of tweed was tweel, or twill, and according to folklore, became tweed only when the word tweels on a letter sent by a Scottish firm to a London merchant was misread as tweed, the name of a river that flows through the area close to the Scottish border. The name stuck.

Tweed comes from Scotland, with the best known being Harris Tweed, first woven in the 18th century by crofters in the Outer Hebrides. In the 1840s it was introduced to the British aristocracy and the cloth was used to make garments for the privileged to wear when hunting, shooting and fishing. In 1909 the Harris Tweed Orb Certification Mark was created to protect against imitations. To qualify, the tweed must be woven on a hand-powered (not electric) loom by the islanders, and made from pure virgin wool dyed and spun in the Outer Hebrides. ▪

Tweed is the epitome of Britishness

Polo mint

Polos are advertised in Britain as 'the Mint with the Hole', and its makers claim that more than 140 of them are eaten every second, but not we assume, by the the same person. They were first produced in 1948 by Rowntree, who were then one of a small number of companies in the UK (including Cadbury of Creme Egg fame) which were started in the 19th century by a Quaker family and run on philanthropic principles. But since 1998 the company has been owned by the Swiss giant Nestlé, who claim to make 38 million Polos every day. They also say it takes the weight of two elephants to press a Polo, though this does seem a rather primitive method of production.

Shaped like a lifebelt (and probably modelled on the American Lifesaver sweet), Polos have been made in other flavours, such as fruit and spearmint, but it is the white mint in a green tube-shaped wrapper that has wormed its way so firmly into British affections. (For a while you could also buy small discs of the hard white mint, which were claimed to be the hole removed from the middle of a Polo mint.)

Consumers of Polos are typically split between 'crunchers', who bite into the hard mint, and 'suckers', who let them dissolve gradually in the mouth. Whether this difference has any psychological or social significance has, as far as we know, not yet been established. However, a Facebook page set up to investigate just this topic suggests that there are slightly more suckers than crunchers, with just over 30,000 suckers recording their preference, compared with 25,000 crunchers.

People often suck a Polo mint to mask the smell of pungent foods like garlic or curry. Sometimes though, sucking a Polo can be covering up something more serious; the shame of a person as they slink home to their partner late at night after drinking with friends, or perhaps after a secret meeting with an illicit lover. ■

They say it takes the weight of two elephants to press a Polo, though this does seem a rather primitive method of production

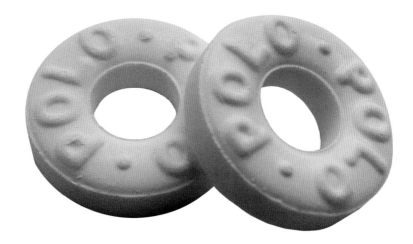

Brompton bike

If you get on any train or bus, or step out onto any busy London street, there is a good chance you will see a Brompton bike. Why are Bromptons so popular? Because they are not just easy to fold up and carry, but also good to ride – and that makes them ideal for busy city commuters. Riders can cycle to the station, fold their bikes up in 30 seconds or less and carry them like a suitcase on to the train, then unfold them again and cycle to their workplaces at the other end.

The Brompton is not the cheapest fold-up bike on the market (the cheapest Brompton model costs £700 and the most expensive over £1,300), nor is it the lightest (although there is a more expensive titanium framed version), but independent tests consistently give it top ratings. One online review concludes: 'These are amazing bikes!' – noting that they can be used not just for short rides to work, but also for shopping, as well as for holidays and longer rides. They are robust and practical, and due to the clever design all the oily bits are on the inside, so riders will not wipe the chain on their clothes when carrying their bikes.

Perhaps the most unusual aspect of Bromptons is that they are still made in the UK, just six miles from Harrods (which is itself located on Brompton Road) in west London. And the company is still British owned and managed. The bikes themselves are sold all over the world, with specially strong sales in Hong Kong, South Korea and Japan. There is no doubt, the company concedes, that it would be cheaper to make the bikes in China, but it is convinced that its customers 'love that the bikes are handmade in London!'

The story of the Brompton has much in common with that of the Dyson vacuum cleaner. The founder of the business, Andrew Ritchie, left university with a degree in Engineering and after a series of other jobs, happened to see the prototype of another manufacturer's folding bike and was immediately convinced he could do better.

With the financial support of some friends he produced the first prototypes in his bedroom which looks out over the Brompton Oratory in South Kensington, London. Like Dyson, he initially thought of licensing his design to one of the more established bike manufacturers, but none of the major makers like Raleigh were interested. So, like Dyson, Andrew Ritchie set about making the bikes himself, also with the help of friends, who pre-ordered 30 bikes from him. Ritchie's big break came when Brompton won the prestigious Best Product award at the 1987 Cyclex exhibition, against some strong international competition.

As Brompton wryly note on their website: 'No one could have dreamt that twenty years later Brompton would be the largest bicycle builder in the UK and Raleigh little more than an importer of kits!' Another point of comparison with Dyson.

Brompton continues to be profitable, producing some 30,000 bikes per year, and it is targeting continued growth in the future on the back of new lightweight models, as well as electric versions. In the UK it is likely to be helped by national campaigns to promote safer cycling and increased use of bikes for short journeys and commuting. ■

'Handmade in London!'

Bayonet light bulb

Everybody thinks they know who invented the first incandescent light bulb. It was Thomas Edison, right? The answer is: maybe. But if we were to ask: who was the first person to file a successful patent for the light bulb, the answer would be clearer. And it wasn't Thomas Edison. It was Joseph Swan (later Sir Joseph Swan), a British physicist and chemist who filed the first patent in 1878. His house, in the north east of England, was the first house anywhere in the world to be lit by electric light. And, in 1881, the Savoy Theatre in London was the first public building in the world to be illuminated entirely by electricity – using Swan's light bulbs, of course.

Edison was much more commercially minded than Swan – and that is perhaps why he is better remembered than his British counterpart. The two inventors went on to set up the Edison & Swan United Electric Light Company, selling lamps made with a cellulose filament that Swan had invented in 1881. Edison went on to patent the Edison

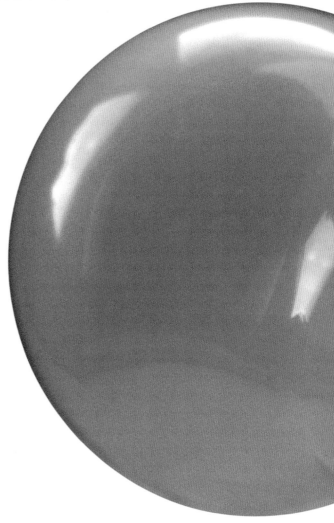

Who patented the first light bulb?
It wasn't Thomas Edison

screw fitting, the type of screw-in bulb that is now used in most parts of the world.

Meanwhile, the bayonet fitting became the British standard and can also be found in other countries such as India, where Britain previously had influence. It is called a bayonet fitting for the simple reason that it is fitted using the same push-and-twist action used by a soldier to fit a bayonet on to a rifle.

As retailers like IKEA have introduced new light designs from abroad, many of which use screw-type fittings, so consumers in Britain have had to accept some change. But just as British drivers continue, unlike most other countries, to drive on the left, so too do they continue to use the bayonet bulb. The cost of changing now would in any case probably be too high.

The shape of the bulb may change as low energy tubes replace the old incandescent technology, but the bayonet still survives. ■

Brown sauce

Brown sauce is a popular accompaniment to the traditional English breakfast and one of the foods that British people living abroad say they miss most.

On the face of it the idea of brown sauce is not very appetising, with the colour's associations with sewers, mud and slurry, and it is true that the strong flavour of brown sauce is not to everyone's taste. It contains vinegar, tomatoes, sweeteners, dates, salt, tamarind, soy sauce, spices and onion extract – an amalgam of ingredients that combine the traditionally British with exotic new discoveries from far-flung parts of what was once the British Empire. A plus side is that the sauce contains no animal products, so is suitable for vegetarians.

The most popular brand of brown sauce is HP Sauce, now owned by the American company HJ Heinz. The original recipe for HP Sauce was created by

Frederick Gibson Garton, a grocer from Nottingham. He registered the name HP Sauce in 1895, claiming that he had heard the sauce was being served in the restaurant in the Houses of Parliament. Whether the story was true or not, it gave his product instant credibility, and ever since then the bottle labels have carried a picture of the Houses of Parliament.

Other companies followed on, launching their own forms of brown sauce, and you will now find many brands on supermarket shelves, including Tiptree, shown here. The popularity of brown sauce grew further in World War One, when it was served to the British troops (no doubt a great way of disguising the taste of the mass-produced slop they had to eat in the trenches).

It gained more publicity in the 1960s when the wife of Prime Minister Harold Wilson revealed that her husband doused his food in it. It turned out later that this was not true, but by then the story had gained so much publicity that brown sauce became known as 'Wilson's gravy'. It seems Wilson was perfectly happy with this as it enhanced his reputation as a man of the people.

The popularity of brown sauce continues to this day, even though we are all supposed to have become accomplished cooks with more sophisticated palates. On the web you will find nostalgic observations from brown sauce lovers and pleas from British expats:

'Love this sauce, I'm from Sheffield, UK, but now living in Boston, USA, I need this for my butties!! Does anyone know where I can buy this?'

'Cheese sarny with HP Sauce OH YES those were the days MMMM!!' ■

'Love this sauce, I'm now living in Boston, USA, I need this for my butties!! '

Dartboard

Britain hosts a World Darts Championship (well, two of them actually) that, rather like baseball's World Series in the USA, is never won by anyone outside its host country. Well, almost never. Just as the Baseball World Series has occasionally allowed a Canadian team (the Toronto Blue Jays) to enter and even to win, so too Britain has from time to time allowed a Dutchman, an Australian or a Canadian to get a look in at darts.

Darts became a popular game in England in the early part of the 20th century and pub landlords were quick to pick up on it as a good way of attracting customers. But there were a few problems to resolve before it could become a major sport. First of all each region in England had its own version of the game, which made it hard to run any kind of national competitions. And then there was the problem of the dartboard itself.

The dartboard is probably a descendant of the original archery target, scaled down for indoor play. Boards were originally made of wood, usually elm, cut from the end of a tree trunk. (The tree rings and radial cracks in the wood probably explain why the dartboard came to be laid out the way it is.) After each day's play the pub landlord would have to soak the wooden

Down at your local pub you can engage in just the same intensive programme as top international darts players

dartboard to heal the holes made by the darts, and to make it resistant to cracking. Even then chunks of wood would sometimes be pulled out of a board when a player extracted his dart.

The solution was presented by a company called Nodor, who still make dartboards to this day. In 1932 they patented a new type of board – the bristle board, which did not crack and left no mark when the dart was pulled out. This new board was, however, quite expensive and did not completely replace the old wooden boards till the 1970s, when Dutch Elm disease destroyed the supply of elm wood and growing affluence made the bristle boards more affordable.

The first television broadcasting of darts started in 1962, but it took some time to take off, attracting over 4 million viewers for the final in 1999. Part of the game's appeal is that the top players are very evidently not athletes, many being overweight and supping a pint of beer between rounds. Down at your local pub you will probably find a dartboard and can engage in the same intensive work-out programme as top international darts players. ▥

English mustard

Comedians love to give visitors to Britain advice on what to expect and how to behave when they visit this country. This includes suggestions along the following lines: All British people know the Queen personally, so be sure to ask them how she is. Always ask the bartender to put ice in your bitter. Don't worry too much about queuing – just push your way to the front. Always be sure to ask your neighbour on the underground about their personal life – British people are always very open to discussing such things with strangers. The mustard is very weak, so you will need to put plenty on your burger, hot dog, or ham sandwich if you want to taste it.

All these pieces of advice can land you in problems, but if you are accustomed to the kind of the yellow mustard sauces served at American baseball venues, for example, then you could be in for

a particularly nasty shock. Just like chillis (and yes we grow the world's hottest chillis too*) English mustard can be deceptively strong. Take too much and you'll be left doubled up with your nose and eyes streaming.

*(At Grantham in Lincolnshire they grow chillis rated at well over 1,000,000 Scoville Heat Units (SHU) compared to around 5,000 for the hottest Jalapeno.)

Mustard is the original 'hot stuff'. No one knows for sure how phrases like 'to cut the mustard' (meaning: to be the best) and 'keen as mustard' (meaning: very enthusiastic) originated, but they both carry a strong and positive meaning. English Mustard is among the strongest in the world, made from mustard flour, water, salt and, sometimes, lemon juice, without the vinegar which makes other mustards rather milder.

There are many brands of English mustard on the market, but Colman's is probably the best known. Started in 1814 in Norwich Colman's quickly grew and took over other producers, including Keen's Mustard. It was about 50 years later that the bull's head was added to the label, and which later became its trade mark.

In 1926 Colman's ran one of the earliest 'teaser' marketing campaigns. The company put posters on London buses with the question 'Has Father Joined the Mustard Club?' but no other details. People rang the bus companies and the newspapers to find out about the club, which eventually released more details about itself. By the time the campaign was wound up in 1933 half a million membership badges had been issued. ■

'Has Father Joined the Mustard Club?'

Hackney carriage

Better known as a London taxi or black cab, the hackney carriage pictured below is as unmistakably British – and as essential a feature of any London street scene – as the red double decker London bus.

The London taxi, like all taxis, is called a hackney carriage because Hackney – a district long since absorbed into London – was once a village famous for breeding horses, including the working horses that were hired out to work the fields, or pull carts and carriages. This is how the term hackney carriage came to be associated with a horse-drawn carriage available for hire, the forerunner of the present-day taxi. Modern taxis are no longer made in the area, though, instead being produced in Coventry.

Some people will tell you that there is still a law, the 1831 Hackney Carriage Act, that requires London taxi drivers to carry a bale of hay in their cabs. Sadly, much as we would love this to be true, the law simply

requires taxi drivers to feed their horses themselves, but if they have no horse they do not have to carry the hay.

All taxi drivers in London have to acquire 'The Knowledge' before they can take to the streets, and you will see motorcyclists tootling round the streets on scooters or small motorbikes with a clipboard on their handlebars. These are trainee taxi drivers preparing to take their test. You might think that satnav would have made The Knowledge unnecessary. It certainly helps, but if you have ever taken a taxi during London rush hour, then you will have come to the value of The Knowledge as your driver dives up small alleyways barely wider than the cab itself and then emerges at the front of the jam. No satnav has yet been invented that can match that kind of local knowledge.

The black cab looks very old fashioned with its upright windscreen, round headlamps and front mudguards. Its shape has not changed radically in the last 40 years. And in an age when almost every new compact car is front-wheel drive, how is it that the taxi still drives via the rear wheels? The answer is that the London taxi is perfectly adapted to its environment.

Watch a black cab do a U-turn in a narrow London street and you will see that it enjoys an unrivalled turning circle. Inside, its flip-down seats and extra space beside the driver allow the flexibility to carry extra passengers or additional luggage. And watch a cab heading out west of London towards Heathrow carrying five people and all their holiday luggage, some of it strapped to the fold-down boot lid: form following function. ∎

Some people will tell you that there is still a law that requires London taxi drivers to carry a bale of hay in their cabs

Tennis racquet

Tennis is of course a global sport. And you can eat strawberries and cream almost anywhere you like. Bring the two together, however, and add in some grass – plus maybe the odd rain shower – and you could not be anywhere other than in Britain, or more precisely at Wimbledon in early July.

For almost 100 years up to the 1970s, all tennis racquets were made of wood, and strings were made from animal gut. Unlike cricket, which established rules to protect the original wood construction, tennis has evolved to allow new technologies, resulting in a much faster and more physically demanding game. Laminated wood construction made racquets stronger until they gave way to aluminium, carbon graphite, ceramics, and titanium, whilst animal gut was replaced by modern synthetic materials.

The modern game of tennis started life in Birmingham, around 1860, and its invention is now generally credited to Major Harry Gem and his friend Augurio Perera. Until that time tennis, or rackets as it was often called, was played indoors, bouncing the ball off walls as in present day squash. It was Gem and Perera who took the game outdoors to the croquet lawn at Gem's

house in Edgbaston and who then founded the world's first lawn tennis club in Leamington Spa in 1872.

In spite of this neither Gem nor Perera is officially credited with inventing the game. That accolade goes to Major Walter Clopton Wingfield, who patented a game he called Sphairistike (from the Greek meaning skill at playing a ball), or Lawn Tennis, in 1874. Luckily it was the name Lawn Tennis rather than Sphairistike that caught on.

It is Clopton's name that appears on the International Tennis Hall of Fame and whose bust stands outside Wimbledon Lawn Tennis Club Museum. Whoever we credit as the inventor, the game soon gained popularity with the middle and upper classes and more clubs quickly sprang up. Wimbledon, or rather The All England Lawn Tennis and Croquet Club, was founded in 1868 and staged its first Lawn Tennis Championship in 1877, initially only for men, but followed just five years later by a competition for women.

Since that time, whilst the game has become more physically demanding for players, Wimbledon has become much easier for spectators. The addition of a removable roof over Wimbledon's Centre Court now allows them to enjoy their strawberries and cream without having to huddle under an umbrella from the occasional rain shower. ▪

Luckily it was the name Lawn Tennis rather than Sphairistike that caught on

London Underground map

Sometimes an object looks so perfect that it is hard to imagine how it could have ever been designed any other way. You wonder what all the fuss is about. The London Underground map is one of those things.

It is only when you see the earlier efforts at mapping the underground that you realise what is so clever about Harry Beck's 1930s design. Previous layouts tried to represent the underground more like a conventional geographical map, as though the ground had been X-rayed. The results were messy. Beck chose instead to use a schematic layout that is more geometric. He used clear colour coding for the different lines, but scale is only approximate.

There are no roads or landmarks. The only concession to what is on the surface is the inclusion of the River Thames.

The result is a clear and much imitated design. The map has evolved as new underground lines have been added to the network, but it is still faithful to the original design. In 2009 Transport for London introduced a map that omitted the river but it had to be withdrawn after numerous complaints.

There are, of course, some drawbacks when you mess with scale, and if you are travelling around London you might want to arm yourself with a street map because some journeys will be quicker on foot, particularly if you take account of the amount of walking you have to do underground. For example, Leicester Square is only 5 minutes' walk from Covent Garden and Charing Cross to Embankment is about the same.

Much as we love the old paper-based tube map, we have to acknowledge that it works just as well on a smartphone, as shown here. And the addition of apps that work out your best route and tell you about hold-ups swings the balance in favour of newer technology. But that takes nothing away from the genius of the original design. ∎

*The results
were messy*

Custard

Custard is made from milk or cream, and egg yolk. It can be a thin pouring sauce (sometimes called *crème anglaise*) or a thick jelly-like mixture of the kind used in custard tarts or slices. Custards baked in pastry were enjoyed as long ago as the Middle Ages, but it was in the 1840s that custard itself really became popular.

That was when Alfred Bird invented custard powder for his wife, who was allergic to eggs. Bird used cornflour instead to thicken the sauce and soon discovered that he had a potential bestseller on his hands. Bird set about marketing it vigourously and Bird's Custard Powder became very successful, its light weight before hydration making it ideal for transportation on ships heading out to the British colonies.

Today British consumers are more likely to buy ready-made custard, which they simply have to heat up and serve. In pubs custard makes a popular dessert, served as an accompaniment to apple crumble or even better: sticky toffee pudding, a sponge made with thick toffee sauce. The kind of dessert you have because, as your grandmother would have said, 'Your eyes are just too big for your stomach.' ■

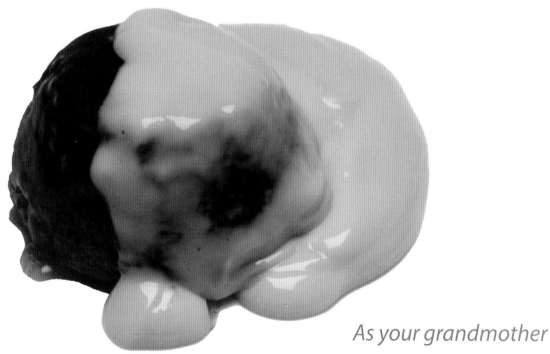

As your grandmother would have said, 'Your eyes are just too big for your stomach'

JCB 3CX

JCB belongs to that small list of companies – another being Hoover – that come to define not just their own product but the whole category in which they operate. The company created the first mechanical digger – sometimes called a backhoe loader – in 1953 and since then JCB has become a generic term covering any tractor that has a bucket at the front and a digger at the back.

Up and down the length of Britain, and all over the world, you will see JCB's distinctive yellow machines excavating foundations on building sites, carving trenches along roads, digging ditches on farms, shifting rocks in quarries, or even clearing rubble after an earthquake. Its current 3CX model shown here is a direct descendant of the iconic 3C model of the 1960s, the original backhoe loader that made JCB's name.

JCB's fastest backhoe loader could reach 140mph

JCB continues to make construction machinery at its Rocester factory in Staffordshire (as well as at a further 17 factories around the globe) and it remains British-owned. It is now one of the world's top three manufacturers of construction equipment, employing 7000 people and selling its products in 150 countries.

This is a far cry from the company started in 1945 by Joseph Cyril Bamford, who gave his initials to the company along with his genius for practical invention. That was the year when he welded together scrap steel to make and sell his first piece of equipment – a farm trailer. But Bamford was not only a gifted engineer. He was also a talented marketer.

He developed the company's crisp black on yellow logo early in its history and maintained it carefully. JCBs are not just highly functional pieces of equipment. Bamford understood his customers and sought to make their lives easier; for example, every 3C came with an electric kettle which could be plugged into the cab. A thoughtful touch.

Bamford always managed to combine the functional with a flair for publicity. One of his party tricks was standing a JCB up on its buckets, with the wheels off the ground, and then driving his car underneath. In the 1980s the company built the JCB GT, a 1300 hp backhoe loader capable of reaching 140 mph. In 2005 the JCB Dieselmax set a land speed record for a diesel-powered car when it was driven at over 350 mph, beating the previous record by over 100 mph.

The JCB now has popular appeal across the whole population. In 2005 Nizlopi reached number one in the UK music charts with the 'JCB' song. Also, at four Diggerland adventure parks across the country both children and adults can now ride on and drive JCBs themselves (under the guidance of trained staff) even if they do not have a driving licence. ∎

Hot and cold taps

Many visitors to Britain are struck by the common use of separate hot and cold taps in the UK. In fact for many visitors to Britain our plumbing seems to be a major source of fascination, particularly if they stay in an older bed and breakfast or hotel.

Even though the first mixer tap was patented as long ago as 1880, most older houses in Britain are still equipped with separate taps, and we even continue to fit them in new houses to this day.

Mostly however the mixer tap has arrived and is common in new kitchens and bathrooms, but many still prefer their taps to be separate. You know where you are with separate taps. No risk of filling your drinking glass with a stream of warm water if you

Better than a strong coffee to wake you on a winter's morning

have a separate cold tap. But be careful. As there is no specified standard layout for fitting the two taps, you cannot be sure which tap is which, unless it is clearly marked. And if you come from southern Europe you may expect 'C' on a tap to tell you that it will produce hot water (C for *chaud*, *caliente* or *caldo*) whereas of course it will be the 'C' for cold tap.

Choose the wrong tap and it will be better than a strong coffee to wake you on a winter's morning. ■

Belisha beacon

The Belisha beacon is an orange flashing globe on top of a black and white striped post, always found either side of zebra crossings (which are pedestrian road crossings marked by black and white stripes painted on the road surface). Probably the most famous zebra crossing in Britain appears on the cover of The Beatles' 1969 *Abbey Road* album, but the Belisha beacons cannot be seen because they are out of sight at the side of the road.

In the early days of motoring pedestrian crossings were simply marked by metal studs across the road. Then, in 1934 the Transport Minister – the wonderfully named Leslie Hore-Belisha – decided that they were not easy enough to see. So he added the distinctive lights and donated half his name to them.

It was only in the early 1950s that the white stripes were painted on the road to create the zebra crossing. For the overseas visitor the critical point is that car drivers are legally required to stop at a zebra crossing, and British motorists are generally good at observing this law. The pedestrian, however, should give traffic plenty of time to stop before crossing.

Many British people are barely aware of the existence of zebra crossings with Belisha beacons. This is partly because they are such a common feature of any urban landscape, but also because many zebra crossings have now been replaced by pelican crossings, the difference being that pelicans use conventional traffic lights, which are activated by the pedestrian pressing a button at the roadside. Toucan, puffin and tiger crossings also exist (once road planners had started the animal theme it seems they couldn't let go of it) but unless you are a cyclist you are unlikely to come across them. ■

*The most famous zebra crossing in Britain?
On the cover of The Beatles' Abbey Road album*

Magnolia paint

*Magnolia is to
British house
decorators
as grass
is to cows*

Britain is a country where owning your own home has been a universal dream for many centuries. The phrase 'the Englishman's home is his castle' (just as true of the Scots and Welsh and of women) dates back to the 17th century when Sir Edward Coke established this as a principle in common law in *The Institutes of the Laws of England*, 1628. Its meaning? Quite simply that their home is every man or woman's refuge, a place where no one can boss them around, where they are free (up to a point, of course) to do as they please.

Even now, after the end of the property boom, there are still TV programmes about 'doing up property' for profit. This usually means preparing a house so that it looks clean, tidy, and offends no one; key to this is the use of Magnolia paint.

A kind of pale pinkish shade – not quite white, not quite peach – Magnolia is to British house decorators as grass is to cows: it is everywhere and they never tire of it.

Every now and then a weekend newspaper colour supplement will run an article in which a designer will present bold new colours. An estate agent will extol the virtues of making your house stand out by selective use of bold colours. There will be spreads showing celebrities proudly showing how they (meaning their interior decorator) have made tasteful use of colour in their expensively decorated luxury home.

The truth, though, is that Britain is one of the most densely populated countries in the world. Most British homes are relatively small. And there is a continuing trend towards more small, single-occupancy flats, so they will probably become smaller still. In a small room bright, deep colours can become oppressive, whereas pale, neutral colours add a sense of space and provide a blank canvas for displaying paintings and large-scale photographs. And the British, for all their creativity in music and the arts, can be very conservative indeed in their domestic tastes. Magnolia paint is here to stay. ■

Road signs

In 2011 the Design Museum in London exasperated some by running an exhibition called 'This is Design', which included a full-size motorway road sign. Those who criticised them for this took the view that such signs are a blight on our landscape and a plague in our streets. It is true that if you go along any urban road in Britain you will indeed be bombarded by signs; signs that warn you to slow down, signs to beware of school children, road works or bends in the road, even signs to look out for a 'new' roundabout that was installed five years ago... In short far too many signs. There is a growing awareness that the proliferation of them needs to be stopped, not just because they are ugly but because drivers cannot absorb all the different messages coming at them.

Back in the late 1950s the problems were rather different. At that time signs were inconsistent and often hard to read; many dated back to the 1920s and looked old fashioned. Two graphic designers, Jock Kinnear and Margaret Calvert, were commissioned to come up with a standardised and modern system of signage, one that could cope with the emerging motorway age.

Their solution was to create two new typefaces: Transport, which is used on most of the current road signs, and Motorway, a variant of Transport which is used on all the distinctive blue signs on British motorways. Where towns and cities on the previous road signs used all capital letters, Kinneir and Calvert chose the same mix of capitals and lower case that you are reading here. They simplified the language used. 'HALT – MAJOR ROAD AHEAD' became simply 'STOP'. The changes were the result of rigorous testing. Signs were propped up against trees around London's Hyde Park and they assessed how easy they were to read.

At the same time they devised a set of graphic symbols that would convey the necessary message quickly and effectively to a driver moving at speed. There was even a little bit of subliminal social suggestion in their approach. The previous sign warning of a nearby school showed a boy in front of a girl, both wearing school hats and carrying books and satchels, the new one shows an older girl leading a smaller boy across the road, and without the hats or satchels. The signs have stood the test of time, with few changes; many have been copied in other countries.

The only sign that Calvert wished she had done differently is the one that people like best: the men at work sign, which shows a man pushing a shovel into a pile of sand (shown here) which inspired an album by the musician Viv Stanshall called *Men Opening Umbrellas Ahead*. Not many road signs have had music written in their honour. ■

Glamping tent

If you are British and over 40 you may have childhood memories of family holidays in which your parents crammed you into the family car along with sleeping bags, pillows, pans and a camp stove, for a long and boring drive into some remote part of the countryside. Once arrived you would all then struggle gamely, in a Force 8 storm, to nail down a flapping expanse of unruly blue canvas, all the while being whipped round the head by flailing guy ropes. Alternatively perhaps your memories take in the distinctive musty smell of a beige-coloured scout or guide tent, or more recently the abandoned battle to pack up your mud-spattered pop-up tent after a music festival.

If so, then you will welcome the new kind of camping experience taking over Britain – Glamorous Camping – or Glamping for short.

Visitors to the Glastonbury festival, for example, no longer have to accept discomfort. Anyone who has £8,000 or so available to spend on the weekend can stay in style, renting a shikar tent (like those used by ancestors of the Maharajah of Jodhpur for hunting trips). The tent accommodates a king-sized bed with Egyptian cotton sheets, duck down duvets and 'jewel spangled Rajasthani covers'. The floors are covered in sheepskin. And no more queuing for the malodorous loos; for a bit more money you can order your own en suite toilet plumbed into the tent for your exclusive use.

But Glamping is not confined to music festivals. All over the country campsites quite unlike those known to our parents are springing up. At Cuckoo Down Farm in Devon, for example, you can rent an 18 m diameter yurt with a wooden floor, furnished with rugs, a double bed, two double sofa beds plus cushions, a coffee table, storage chests and a wood-burning stove. And not to forget: an eco-friendly compost toilet as well. Or if you still feel that a night under canvas is too demanding there are now a wide range of traditional gypsy caravans to hire for the week around the country.

For your wedding you can now choose to hold the happy event in a marquee and then employ Tobyn Cleeves' Hotel Bell Tent service to provide four or five metre diameter luxury bell tents, like the one pictured here, for your guests to sleep in, free of the worries of getting back to a hotel after a day of celebration.

Our parents would be speechless at how soft we have become. ■

…a king size bed with Egyptian cotton sheets, duck down duvets… Our parents would be speechless at how soft we have become

Range Rover

Over its 40 year life the Range Rover has evolved from a functional vehicle into an exclusive style icon that is respected and desired all over the world. It is true that some green campaigners dismiss it as a symbol of excess – a gas-guzzling monster, or a 'Chelsea tractor' – that represents the worst of conspicuous consumption in an age when they say we should be conserving resources, but there is no doubt that it remains a universally acknowledged status symbol. More energy efficient technologies promise to address the environmental criticisms in the near future.

Today's Range Rover is very different from the car that was launched in 1970. The original car had vinyl seats and rubber mats on the floor. It was designed to be a working vehicle on a farm or estate in the morning, climbing effortlessly over fields, hills and rough ground, and a comfortable road vehicle in the afternoon; at home in both town and country, and above all: practical. Shortly after it was launched in 1970, it appeared in an exhibition at the Louvre, where it was described as an 'exemplary work of industrial design'.

'An exemplary work of industrial design'

It was later that the car acquired its cachet of luxury, with burr walnut veneers, leather seats and deep pile carpets. Many credit the Range Rover with being the first luxury SUV (Sports Utility Vehicle), though the Jeep Wagoneer arguably pioneered that category some years before the first Range Rover appeared.

The Rover Car Company, the creator of the original Land Rover, which is now known as the Land Rover Defender, had been experimenting with ideas for an alternative model as far back as 1951. Nothing came of it until 1966 when the concept was revisited, with the project cloaked in secrecy. They even formed a new company, named Velar, and registered pre-production cars under that name to avoid any links to Land Rover itself.

Bearing out the Range Rover's ruggedness and off-road ability it immediately became the vehicle of choice for long-distance overland expeditions including the 1972 British Trans-Americas Expedition. In this event the Range Rover crossed North and South America, traversing the notorious Darien Gap where there were no roads. It also became a popular vehicle, together with other Land Rover off-roaders, in the Camel Trophy, which ran from 1980 to 2000.

Today the Range Rover remains a highly competent off-road vehicle, with an exceptional capability to negotiate difficult terrain, even though most drivers never tackle more than the occasional snow-covered road or the pot-holed track. And, through its many driver aids, owners report that it is also surprisingly easy to drive in cities as well. Now joined by a smaller alternative, the Evoque, the Range Rover brand continues to expand. Future developments are likely to include hybrid technology – but the off-road capability will remain. ∎

Cricket bat and ball

We like rules in Britain – just as long as we get to draw them up and can change them whenever we want.

Perhaps that is why there are so many sports – like football, rugby, darts, snooker and tennis – that we have created or formalised over the last four centuries. The English language is littered with phrases that reflect our love of rules in sport, such as: 'fair play' (French 'le fair-play'), 'a level playing field' and 'that's just not cricket!' – the latter used when the speaker is confronted by something they consider to be unfair.

The laws of cricket date back to 1788 and were drawn up by the Marylebone Cricket Club (MCC). There are 42 of them in total, each covering a different aspect of the game. So, for example, Law 5 specifies the weight and size of the ball, while Law 6 prescribes the dimensions of the bat. It also states that the bat must be made only of wood and usually that wood will be white willow, which is treated with linseed oil to protect it.

The cricket bat has evolved over the centuries and until 1979 no one thought it necessary to spell out that it should be made of wood, but in that year an Australian player, Dennis Lillee, tried to use an aluminium bat, which was promptly outlawed. Similar changes to the laws have been made to restrict the use of other technical enhancements such as carbon fibre in the handle. This contrasts strongly with tennis, where wood has long since been superseded by more advanced materials.

The ball is also unique, with its leather surface and raised welt of stitching. Being able to judge the state of the ball and how it will behave on a given pitch as the game progresses is a key part of the skill of the game.

Law 42 in cricket captures the British attitude to rules in sport perfectly. It puts the responsibility for ensuring fairness squarely on the shoulders of the team captains, but also states that the umpires are the sole judges of fair and unfair play. Not just that, but if either umpire (there are always two) considers an action to be unfair, even if it is not covered by the laws of cricket, then he can intervene.

There is plenty of evidence that adherence to the sporting traditions of cricket is weakening, with recent stories of match fixing and ball tampering showing that the big money in all international sports today makes distortion of the rules for profit all the more tempting and the authorities have struggled to keep up with such abuses. ■

We like rules in Britain just as long as we can change them whenever we want

Rolls-Royce Phantom

Rolls-Royce is a name that whispers luxury, prestige and quality. Where a Ferrari is like an Italian tenor personifying style and speed, Rolls-Royce is the dignified aristocrat who quietly assumes privilege as a right. It is possible to love a Rolls-Royce and hate it at the same time; admire its engineering excellence, delight in its understated elegance; yet despise the exclusivity and the unwarranted assumptions of superiority that it conveys on its owner.

All over the world the name Rolls-Royce is used quite simply to mean 'the best'. In 1958 the advertising agency Ogilvy & Mather produced an ad for the Rolls-Royce Silver Cloud whose headline read: 'At

60 miles an hour the loudest noise comes from the electric clock.' It went on to talk about the acoustic tuning of the exhaust system, the five coats of primer and nine coats of paint (each layer hand-finished), the French walnut used in the picnic table and the options list which included hot and cold water, a bed and an espresso coffee machine...

At that time, according to the ad, you could buy a Rolls-Royce for $13,995 (before options). Today the latest Phantom will cost you around $450,000, but if you cannot afford that, do not worry. You could always

'Whatever is rightly done, however humble, is noble.'

choose the Rolls-Royce Ghost instead, available for a more reasonable $300,000.

Of course you will not see many Rolls-Royces on the road in Britain. They turn heads there just as much as they do in New York, Beijing or Tokyo. But perhaps they do look a bit more at home in a British city or landscape. For ten years in the 1920s Rolls-Royce built cars in Springfield, Massachusetts, but customers wanted them to be made in Britain, so they closed the factory. The cars are now made at a new factory which opened in 2003 at Goodwood in Sussex, near to the historic Goodwood motor and horse racing tracks and to Goodwood House, the stately home of the Dukes of Richmond for several centuries. This is Rolls-Royce's homeland.

Charles Rolls and Henry Royce met in 1904. Rolls was an enthusiast of cars and aeroplanes – relishing the speed and excitement that they offered to the wealthy in those pioneering days. He provided the finance and business acumen needed, but died in 1910 in a flying accident when the tail broke off his plane. Royce was the engineering brains, dedicated to excellence. His commitment is summed up in his motto: 'Whatever is rightly done, however humble, is noble'. It was Royce who carried on and built the business, including taking it into the making of aero engines, outliving his business partner by over 20 years. ■

David Mellor cutlery

For more than two centuries Sheffield has been a centre for the manufacture of steel and cutlery.

Thomas Boulsover invented Sheffield plate (silver-plated copper) there in the early 18th century. In the 1740s Benjamin Huntsman discovered the crucible technique, which was superseded a century later by the Bessemer converter.

Stainless steel was perfected by Harry Brearley in Sheffield around 1913. Through to the 1980s Sheffield continued to be a centre for the development of modern high-strength low-alloy steels. At its peak more than half the population of Sheffield was involved in the steel and cutlery industries, but from the 1980s on it has struggled to compete with emerging low cost centres of production around the world.

This industrial decline was captured in the 1997 film *The Full Monty*. Set in Sheffield, it depicted the fortunes of six unemployed men, most of them ex-steel workers, who form a group of strippers. Though it was a comedy, *The Full Monty* touched a nerve as it portrayed a community struggling to recover from the decline of a once major industry.

There are, however, some businesses that have survived: companies that have adapted and focused on the higher added value ends of their markets. One is Forgemasters, founded in 1805, which enjoys a global reputation for producing large complex steel forgings and castings.

Another is David Mellor Design. The founder of the company, David Mellor was born in Sheffield in 1930 and made his name in cutlery, but he was also a talented designer of other products, with credits for furniture, tools, ecclesiastical silver and even traffic lights, a bus shelter and a square post box.

Mellor's earliest range of cutlery, Pride, was designed when he was a student at the Royal College of Art in the 1950s and remains in production to this day. Another range, English, was originally made as a commission for No. 10 Downing Street who required cutlery for ceremonial dining.

Not all of Mellor's designs were successful. His square post box, designed in 1966, had many practical features, for example a system that allowed quick emptying of the box by the postman. The public rebelled, however, more comfortable with the circular pillar box, and Mellor's square boxes were withdrawn after only 200 had been installed. His traffic lights proved much more successful, and his design is still in use today.

Cutlery, however, was always his main interest and by concentrating on making knives, forks and spoons for a relatively small, affluent, design-oriented market he was able to survive and prosper where others succumbed to competition from imported low-cost cutlery. London, shown here, is one of the company's most recent designs. ∎

More than half the population of Sheffield was involved in the steel and cutlery industries

Guy Fawkes mask

The fifth of November is known as Guy Fawkes Night, or Bonfire Night, and in cities, towns and villages across Britain communities get together to light a bonfire and set off fireworks. On the top of each bonfire will be a guy – a stuffed dummy dressed to resemble Guy Fawkes, a man who died over 400 years ago. Many of the people who attend their local bonfire and fireworks display may have little idea who he was or why we remember him. For them, it is just a good family night out as winter sets in. It acts as a warm-up for Christmas, which follows just a few weeks later.

Guy Fawkes was a member of a group of English Catholics who plotted to blow up the Houses of Parliament and kill King James I in 1605. Unfortunately for Fawkes, he was captured while guarding the stockpile of gunpowder in the space under the Palace of Westminster, and he was sentenced to be hanged. On 5 November 1605 Londoners were encouraged to celebrate the King's escape from assassination by lighting bonfires, and every 5 November from that day on was marked as a day of thanksgiving for 'the joyful day of deliverance'. Although there were in total thirteen conspirators, only Guy Fawkes is remembered today.

Part of the tradition – though now not practised as often – includes children making their own guy by stuffing straw or newspaper into old clothes and making a mask for it, then requesting passers-by to give a 'penny for the guy'. As inflation eroded the value of a penny this increased to a pound before the tradition started to die away.

The anti-hero in the graphic novel *V for Vendetta* uses a Guy Fawkes mask as he battles against a fictional fascist state, and it is that image that is used by anti-Wall Street protesters, presumably because they seek, like Guy Fawkes, to shake the foundations of the Establishment. Ironically the *V for Vendetta* image is now owned by Time Warner, a major global media company, and each mask bought by an anti-establishment protester pays a royalty to them. ■

Each mask bought by an anti-establishment protester pays a royalty to a major global media company

Brogue shoe

The holes in the leather were originally included to allow water to drain from the shoes when the wearer crossed a bog

The brogue is a style of shoe whose main distinguishing characteristic is small holes punched into the leather uppers. It is a sturdy piece of footwear, originally from Scotland or Ireland, and the word comes from the Gaelic for shoe. Some claim that the holes in the leather were originally included to allow water to drain from them when the wearer crossed wet terrain such as a bog, but it is hard to see quite how this works. If you put holes in the top but not the bottom, would this not just let the water in... but not out? Whether it was once true or not, the holes are now purely decorative and a brogue will be as water-resistant as any other shoe.

To begin with brogues were simply regarded as practical, strong, outdoor, country walking-shoes mainly intended for men, but over time they have become acceptable as smart shoes for use at social or business occasions, and ranges have been extended to include styles for women. If you want to master the brogue you will have to get to grips with several styles: full brogues, semi-brogues, quarter brogues and longwing brogues, with four styles of closure: oxford, derby, ghillie and monk strap. Or you could just pick some you like.

Britain has a strong tradition of shoe manufacture mainly centred on the East Midlands around Northampton. Many of the long-established companies have now closed or been sold to foreign buyers, but a few survive. Loake, founded in 1880, continues to operate as a family-owned business, making brogues and other shoe styles at its Kettering factory; Joseph Cheaney & Sons, another family-owned business set up in the 1880s, continues to make brogues and other shoes in its factory in the small market town of Desborough; Grenson started in 1866; and Sanders & Sanders, founded in 1873, also continues to thrive.

What each has in common is a focus on high-quality shoes which transcend fashion or fad, the kind of shoes favoured by wearers who buy them even in recessions. Though traditional styles still predominate, some of these long-established makers are looking to update and develop their ranges. Grenson, under its new CEO and Creative Director Tim Little, is setting up its own stores and forging collaborations with other fashion companies and designers to develop new product lines – still building on the tradition of the brogue. ▪

Bagpipes

If you are not a fan then there are just two types of bagpipe: the deafening and the not-quite-so-loud. Or to put it another way: mouth-blown pipes like the Great Highland Bagpipes shown here, which are best played outdoors (unless, as one expert on celtic musical instruments put it, you happen to live in an aircraft hangar); and their smaller cousins: Parlour Pipes, which can be played indoors.

Bagpipes, in a wide variety of different designs, can be found all over the world, including – no doubt to the horror of many Scots – in England, where there are carvings of pipers playing their instruments found in many old cathedrals. But, whereas in England the bagpiping traditions are no longer maintained very strongly, in Scotland they continue to thrive.

There are more than 250 types of bagpipes played around the world today, from Sweden to China. Indeed the first documented bagpipe was found not in Scotland, but in Turkey, and dates back to 1000 BC.

In spite of this it is Scotland's Great Highland Bagpipes that are the most renowned. So much so that it is hard to think about bagpipes without also picturing a Scottish pipe band wearing kilts, sporrans, thick socks, tassels and yards of tartan. And it is only in Scotland that they are used in a military manner; bagpipes in other countries are usually used to accompany dancing.

Whilst the tradition of piping goes back a long time in Scotland, the Great Highland bagpipe is a more recent invention, dating from the early 1800s. Scholars have even suggested that some of the Highland bagpipes in Scottish museums, which are officially associated with major events in Scottish history from the 18th century or earlier, are actually fakes. And, even more bizarrely it seems that the English have played a key part in raising the status of the bagpipes. In 1843 Queen Victoria appointed a 'personal piper to the sovereign'. His job, it seems, was to play the bagpipes under her window at a set time of the day whenever she was in any of her official residences in England or Scotland. This tradition continues today whenever the present Queen is in residence. ∎

Queen Victoria appointed a 'personal piper to the sovereign'

Argos catalogue

'The laminated book of dreams'

To most people outside Britain Argos is an ancient city in Greece whose history stretches back to 5000 BC, which rivalled Sparta in its heyday and which is famous for its ancient temple: the Heraion of Argos.

To anyone living in Britain since 1973 Argos is a shop found on most British high streets, famous for its weighty literary tome: the richly illustrated catalogue of Argos.

When Argos opened its first shop 40 years ago the concept was revolutionary for British consumers. Instead of displaying goods in its windows and around the shop, Argos kept all the products in boxes in a warehouse at the back of the store and customers chose from a catalogue, taking their order on a slip of paper to the counter, then waiting for the item to be collected from the warehouse. Argos saved on floor space and so could carry more products than other shops. Competitive pricing helped to secure their place on the high street.

Over the years the Argos catalogue has charted the shift in consumer tastes and technologies, from typewriters, Polaroid cameras and Spectrum computers – all now long gone – through Sony Walkman, video players and compact sun beds to the consumer toys of today – Apple iPads and BlackBerrys, which will soon in turn look quaint and unsophisticated.

The Argos catalogue once graced the shelves of most British homes, but today its customers are just as likely to go online to search for what they want. The Argos website is one of the most heavily used in the country with millions of hits every month, popular because buyers can check to see if the product is in stock at their local store and reserve it for collection.

For many, however, the twice yearly Argos catalogue, with more than 20,000 desirable consumer items in each, is irresistible. Referred to fondly by comedian Bill Bailey as 'the laminated book of dreams, plastic-covered to protect it from the tears of joy' shed by its grateful users, the Argos catalogue will be sadly missed if one day it is completely replaced by its online equivalent.

For the moment those of us who love to handle objects, to turn pages, to hear, touch and smell paper, will continue to cherish it and hope it can survive. ■

Mr Whippy ice cream van

Until the 1960s almost the only way to eat ice cream at home was by buying it from an ice cream van. These vans would tour the suburban streets of Britain playing a tinny version of 'Greensleeves' through some cheap speakers. And even when homeowners started to acquire freezers, ice cream vans continued to roam the residential streets on summer evenings and at weekends. Their plinky plonk music carries a nostalgic magic for anyone who was a child at that time.

The ice cream van survives to this day, but is now more likely to be found at a sporting event, at a show or at the seaside, than it is touring suburban streets in search of business. In spite of this, though, they are still a regular sight and children still respond to their chimes with the same excitement that their parents did.

The Mr Whippy van is special because it not only sells pre-packaged ice cream and lollies, but also the kind of soft ice cream that is pumped from a machine directly into a cone, topped off with a Cadbury flake to create an ice cream known universally as a 99. This kind of soft ice cream was developed by a research team that reputedly included Margaret Thatcher – in the days when she was a chemist rather than Prime Minister.

The Mr Whippy van shown here is a restored 1950s van still selling 99s today in the Leeds area of northern England. ∎

Children still respond to their chimes with excitement

Dog poo bin

The British love their pets, and most of all their cats and dogs. There are now 17 million of them in Britain – 10 million cats and 7 million dogs – equivalent to more than one for every four people, and that is before you add in pet rabbits, mice, guinea pigs, hamsters, snakes and other assorted pets. The pet food market alone is worth £2 billion a year and rising.

One in four of all cats and dogs is now reckoned to be overweight – not unlike many of their owners. Not just that, but more and more owners in Britain are treating their dogs like people, so apart from overfeeding them, they are pampering them with all kinds of luxuries – 'super premium foods' such as venison or rabbit – gourmet meat dishes sold not in tins but in attractive plastic bowls, as well as soft bedding, clothing, travel accessories... You name it, you can buy it for your dog.

For Christmas, owners can treat their dogs to a Christmas hamper containing a dog toy (with squeaker), a frisbee, a Christmas-themed ball, various things to chew, after-dinner mints and Christmas tarts – all in a nice gift box, with a message attached. And for that formal occasion, why not treat your dog to a collar in the form of a spotted bow tie?

Since 1891 Britain has been the home of what claims to be the world's largest dog show – Crufts – held every March in Birmingham. Hosting 28,000 dogs, it allows owners and breeders to compete for the coveted 'Best in Breed' award.

Not surprisingly the obsessive British love of dogs, and the large number of overfed pets that British people now own, present some unique problems. One of the biggest is that they produce an estimated 1,000 tonnes of dog poo every day. The problem of dog dirt on the streets became so bad that in 2005 the government passed a new law, The Clean Neighbourhoods and Environment Act. This law obliges dog owners to clean up after their pets, giving rise to the dog poo bag – a small, usually black, plastic bag – and the dog poo bin, a relatively recent addition to many of Britain's streets, into which owners should deposit the used bags. Owners who fail to clear up are liable to a steep fine. ■

*7 million dogs =
1,000 tonnes of dog
poo every day*

Red pillar box

The red pillar box is the traditional free-standing post box used in the UK. It is one of the most enduring everyday designs on our streets. The first ones were installed in the Channel Islands in 1852 and were soon adopted across mainland Britain. Before that time anyone wanting to post a letter would have had to take it to a special receiving house or post office. Later designs included a Time of Collection (TOC) plaque, which continues to this day.

There have been a number of different designs over the years – some square, some with six or eight sides, some oval, one design like a fluted Greek column; but the most common, the National Standard Design, is cylindrical with a domed top. Attempts to modernise the design in the 1960s were not well-received by the public and most were withdrawn leaving the older designs in place.

Like all everyday icons, the red pillar box has suffered its fair share of abuse, from daily attack by dogs cocking a leg at its base to schoolchildren posting unpleasant substances or lit matches through its narrow slot. Worse still, the post box has been the frequent target of protests against the government of the day. In 1912 the Suffragette Emily Richardson (who was to die the following year when she threw herself under the King's horse during the Epsom Derby) was imprisoned for ten months for setting fire to post boxes.

In 1939 the Irish Republican Army (IRA) embarked on a short-lived campaign to sabotage the British economy by posting letter bombs inside letter boxes in London, Birmingham and Manchester. There is no record of any deaths resulting from these bombs. The cast iron construction of the pillar box, with its deep foundations, makes it extremely strong. So much so that when the IRA detonated a large bomb in the centre of Manchester in 1996 there was considerable damage to surrounding buildings but the Victorian pillar box, installed in 1887, survived without damage. ■

The red pillar box has suffered its fair share of abuse

Morris dancers' bells and hat

Morris dancing tends to be treated by some in England as a bit of a joke. Whereas it is perfectly acceptable in Scotland for grown men to put on skirts and prance around on one leg with their hands on their hips, somehow morris dancing is seen by many English as slightly absurd, embarrassing even. And yet morris dancing probably has an even longer history in England than highland dance does in Scotland.

The word morris comes from the French *morisque* or Flemish *morisch*; the earliest historical record of morris dancing dates back to 1448 and it was already considered an ancient form of dance by Elizabethan times. In the winter of 1600 the Shakespearean actor William Kemp morris-danced from London to Norwich, a distance of well over 100 miles, drawing out large welcoming crowds along the way. He later chronicled this in his *Nine Daies Wonder*, subtitled: 'Performed in a dance from London to Norwich. Containing the pleasure, pains and kind entertainment of William Kemp between London and that City in his late Morrice.'

'Pleasure, pains and kind entertainment'

The costumes and objects used in dancing vary from region to region. The hat and bells shown here are those worn by the Adlington Morris Men in Cheshire, the bells being worn round the calves, along with a criss-cross ribbon worn across the chest, known as a baldric. Morris dances may feature waved handkerchiefs or sticks, or in some cases swords.

Mummers plays, often performed during winter months by morris dancing teams (or sides, as they are known) introduce a whole new field of costumes: elaborate headgear, masks and uniforms. The kind of characters you would expect to see in a mummers play include: St George, a Turkish Knight, a red-coated soldier and a miracle-working doctor who can bring the dead back to life, each with their own elaborate costume.

The fortunes of morris dancing have risen and fallen, prospering in villages and then declining during the Industrial Revolution as people moved into the cities in search of work. It recovered again when Queen Victoria celebrated her Golden Jubilee in 1887 but then declined once more after World War One following the deaths of so many of its young performers, only to recover once more in the 1960s and 70s when interest in folk music and customs was renewed. For all the jokes people make about morris dancers, people do still love to see them, and groups are always in great demand at local festivities, especially through the summer months. ∎

Cadbury's Creme Egg

Every year in the weeks leading up to Easter, shops all over Britain fill up with chocolate Easter eggs. The association of eggs with the Easter festival is not uniquely British. In fact it is probably stronger in eastern Europe – where a tradition of painting real and wooden eggs dates back centuries. But when it comes to chocolate Easter eggs, Britain leads the way, and a classic example is the Cadbury's Creme Egg.

The Creme Egg is a chocolate egg whose thick shell contains a gooey white and yellow fondant filling, resembling the white and yolk of a real egg. The makers claim that Creme Eggs are the best-selling confectionery item in the UK between New Year's Day and Easter (the only time when they are officially sold), with annual sales in the UK in excess of 200 million, or more than three for every person in the country.

If you piled all the Creme Eggs eaten on top of one another you would have a heap of eggs ten times higher than Mount Everest – and quite a bit tougher to climb. The whole worldwide production of Creme Eggs is made at one factory, in the Bournville area of Birmingham.

Introduced in 1963, the Creme Egg has featured in a number of striking advertising campaigns, including 'How do you eat yours?', for which Cadbury carried out research into how people ate their Creme Eggs. (It seems that 53 per cent bit off the top, licked out the contents and then ate the chocolate, while 20 per cent bit straight into it and almost as many used their forefinger to scoop out the creme.)

When Cadbury was recently sold to the American company Kraft there was a great outcry in Britain. The *Guardian* newspaper ran the

A pile ten times higher than Everest

headline 'Cadbury deal turns Bournville to Mournville'. The reason? Cadbury and its chocolate holds a special place in many British people's hearts and they faced with horror the prospect of the company being sold to a giant US corporation. Cadbury's exalted status is no doubt due in part to warm childhood memories of eating its Dairy Milk chocolate. But it also has something to do with the history of the company.

Started in 1824 by John Cadbury, the business grew quickly. Cadbury was not just an able businessman but also a Quaker and, like many members of non-conformist Christian groups at that time, was prevented from attending university and so turned his energy and intellect towards

business instead. Having very strict moral principles he rejected alcohol and insisted on selling products of high purity and to the correct measure (at a time when this was not always the case). He also believed it was the duty of all men to help their neighbours, and he provided pensions and medical care for his employees and their families long before this became common practice.

In Bournville in Birmingham he built a village of attractive, well-built homes for his workers, each with a garden to enable them to grow vegetables. Now controlled by the Bournville Trust and entirely separate from the Cadbury company, Bournville remains a model of town planning to this day.

John Cadbury's Victorian model of philanthropic business dealings is not unique. Another Quaker chocolate maker, Rowntree, (now also foreign owned – by Nestlé) followed similar philanthropic principles, but Cadbury led the way, and that above all is why it remains such a respected name in Britain. ■

Pantomime dame's costume

Pantomime is a very British form of entertainment. Traditionally performed at Christmas time, pantomime is a popular form of theatre for family audiences. Based loosely on a traditional fairy tale like Cinderella or Snow White, it will always include the following ingredients: music, songs, dancing, clowning around, cross-dressing, slapstick, topical jokes, audience participation, some traditional catch phrases, and a bit of mild sexual innuendo.

Children soon learn to participate in the rituals of pantomime, which include booing at the villain (there is always a baddy); and at some point the characters on stage will engage in an argument that involves one character shouting 'Oh yes it is!' and another shouting 'Oh no it isn't!' with support from the audience. The slapstick will usually include one character hiding behind the other with the audience shouting out 'He's behind you!'

The pantomime dame is the key player in the whole experience. A good dame is the anchor for a successful pantomime, and she will always be played by a man. To add comic effect she wears huge brightly coloured dresses stuffed with masses of padding to create a 'fuller figure', visible frilly underwear, topped off with lashings of make-up on her face... and an extravagant coloured wig. In short: a man who is so obviously trying to play a woman that no one could possibly think she really was a woman. Quite why the pantomime dame is played by a man (and the male hero by a woman) no one really knows, though it may date from Shakespearean times when women did not appear on stage. Whatever the explanation, this playful form of cross-dressing is all part of the fun.

The dame will invariably have several costumes to wear during a performance, together with handbags, feather dusters and any other accessory that can raise a laugh from the audience. By the time the panto reaches its finale her costume will have reached a peak of over-the-top extravagance, and by this time the dame will have helped overcome the villain and, if she is lucky, have found herself a husband as well. ■

'Oh yes it is!'

'Oh no it isn't!'

Barrister's wig

For hundreds of years British judges and lawyers have worn a hat or wig on their heads when in court. In early Tudor times it was a black flat bonnet or cap, but they started wearing wigs around 1680, 20 years after Charles II returned to England from exile in France, bringing the fashion with him. The word wig itself is short for periwig, derived from the French word for a wig, *perruque*.

Wigs had been popular in the French court and so became associated with the ruling classes. Courtiers would compete with one another to wear the most extravagant wigs and even today we use the term 'bigwig' to describe someone who is particularly important, or at least thinks they are. The use of wigs at that (less hygenic) time was probably associated with covering up hair loss, dandruff or unattractive scalp conditions.

For 150 years the legal wig was usually of powdered white or grey hair, which needed a lot of care – curling,

perfuming and powdering – to keep it in usable condition. In 1822 Humphrey Ravenscroft invented a legal wig made of pale horsehair that was much easier to maintain and look after, and the firm of Ede & Ravenscroft still makes the wigs worn by barristers and judges in court today.

Wigs ceased to be fashionable in society at large by 1800, but they have continued to be used in the British legal profession (and in countries whose legal systems are based on the British system of law). Quite why this is so is unclear. One view says that the wig – and its associated robes – provide a way to differentiate the judge and lawyers from others attending court. Perhaps they also convey a sense of learning, experience and responsibility in their wearers, separating them from their everyday identities. There have been more recent efforts to do away with them but, even though the wigs are often scratchy and uncomfortable, British lawyers seem to be very reluctant to give up on them. ▥

Lawyers seem to be very reluctant to give up their wigs

'Queue this way' sign

The British tend to be pretty stoic, a quality that has seen them through some difficult times, like the dark days of World War Two when defeat looked likely and food was short. They also have a strong sense of justice, sometimes referred to as a belief in 'fair play', no doubt related to their fondness for creating sports like cricket, football and rugby and drawing up the rules by which they are run. Bring those two things – stoicism and a sense of fairness – together and you get an explanation for the British fondness for queuing.

It is not that they like to be kept waiting any more than anyone else. Indeed, a recent survey by a division of the mobile phone company O2 suggested that the British are much less willing to wait than they used to be, with most people giving up after six minutes if kept waiting on the phone and complaining if not served in a restaurant within thirteen minutes.

For most British people it is simply that they like to have things well ordered and as stress-free as possible. The simple principle that if you arrive first then it is fair that you get served first ensures this – provided, of course, that everyone else plays by the same rules.

The Times writer Matt Rudd decided to report on the Royal wedding in 2011 by joining the crowds lined up along the Mall in front of Buckingham Palace. After waiting in an orderly line-up for 21 hours there was suddenly a stampede of people from behind him, including two Americans who, riding roughshod over Rudd's British sensibilities, elbowed their way past him, noting to one another that 'the trouble with these Brits is that they don't know how to push to the front'. Disgusted, he set off home missing the royal couple's balcony kiss. ∎

'The trouble with these Brits is that they don't know how to push to the front'

Fulton umbrella

Arnold Fulton was an engineer and inventor who started making umbrellas in 1956 in London, and the company he founded has now grown to be the largest supplier of umbrellas in the UK. Its current range includes a wide variety of different umbrellas – golf, folding, men's, women's and traditional walking umbrellas, as well as the more colourful designer-style range, one of which is shown here – taken from Fulton's Morris & Co collection. The Duke and Duchess of Cambridge gave publicity to Fulton's see-through, or 'bird cage', umbrella when they huddled together under one on their way into the London premiere of the film *War Horse*.

The umbrella, sometimes also referred to as a 'brolly', is not a British invention – although a British inventor, Samuel Fox, did patent the first wire-frame collapsible umbrella in 1842. References to umbrellas have been found in China dating back to earlier than 200 BC (including some amongst the Terracotta Warriors at X'ian), as well as in documents found in the Middle East and Greece. Mostly these were parasols (the word umbrella derives from the Latin for shade), but in Britain it has to be said they are more likely to be used to protect from that regular feature of the British climate – rain.

The umbrella only started to be used in Britain in the 1750s, initially viewed with some suspicion and dismissed as a French fashion. However, its practical benefits soon outweighed any doubts. The traditional image of the London city gent is of a tall man in a bowler hat, pinstripe Savile Row suit with a furled long black umbrella hooked over his arm. But much has changed over the last 50 years. The bowler hat has gone, the typical City worker is likely to be more casually dressed than their New York counterpart, and the umbrella may well be a compact version.

Because of the British climate the umbrella will continue to play an essential part in British life, but along the way it has also been transformed from a simple and functional black 'object' into an aspirational fashion accessory. ▨

*The umbrella was initially
viewed with some suspicion and
dismissed as a French fashion*

Full English breakfast

Depending on where you are staying in Britain you may be offered a Full English, a Full Scottish or a Full Welsh breakfast; or, if you are in Ireland: an Ulster Fry or Full Irish. With a few regional variations they are usually one and the same thing.

The Full English will include some or all of the following: fried egg, bacon, sausage, fried bread, fried mushrooms and grilled tomato, with the possible option of black pudding (especially in northern England), haggis (Scotland), laverbread (Wales), as well as hash browns and baked beans. This may be preceded by porridge (especially in Scotland) or cereals, and should be followed by toast and chunky orange marmalade if you are to do the job properly. And wash it all down with a mug of strong English Breakfast tea (or coffee if you insist).

This can of course end up being a very substantial meal, which will probably keep you going till lunchtime at least. Approach it by following the old proverb: 'Breakfast like a King, lunch like a Prince, dine like a poor man' and you will be fine.

To be clear this is not the typical British person's daily breakfast. Half the working population admit that they do not eat breakfast at all, grabbing a snack later on instead.

The Full English is a treat saved up for times when they are staying at a hotel or Bed and Breakfast. Nothing can compare with a nice lie-in followed by an English breakfast – cooked by someone else of course. Cooking it yourself at home on a weekday? Not likely. ■

Breakfast like a King, lunch like a Prince,

dine like a poor man

Royal Mail rubber band

Some have suggested that the dropped red rubber band is the Royal Mail's equivalent of a dog weeing on a tree

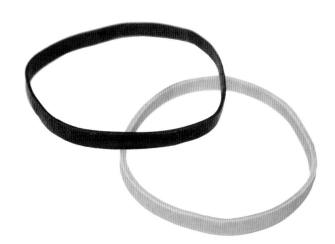

It was a Briton, Stephen Perry, who invented the first rubber band. He patented it on 17 March 1845. His invention is one of the 'hidden heroes' of everyday life: a deceptively simple object that, like the paper clip, and adhesive tape, makes our lives easier though most of us take it for granted.

If you walk around the streets of any British town and glance at the ground you will notice rubber bands lying on the pavement. Carry on and you will soon find yourself discovering more, on the street, in driveways, under cars. You might imagine that Britain is so proud of its invention that it has taken to sprinkling them everywhere. A more likely explanation, however, is that they have been dropped by postmen.

In 2004 the Royal Mail introduced biodegradable rubber bands, using them to bundle letters together for delivery, and it was soon getting through some 800 million of them a year. Not surprising, then, that a fair number ended up on the streets. In 2005, stung by criticism about the number of rubber bands littering British towns and cities, it had the bright idea of using *red* bands instead of the usual brown, hoping that postmen would see them more easily and so pick them up.

Sadly that was not what happened. The postmen continued to drop them in large numbers, but, because they were red, everyone else noticed them too. This led to much light-hearted speculation in the newspapers and on the radio about the possible reasons why so many red rubber bands were appearing on British streets.

Some wondered if the discarded rubber band was the Royal Mail's equivalent of a dog weeing on a tree: to mark out their territory. It was suggested that perhaps they wanted to scare off the new privately-operated couriers by showing them that the Royal Mail had already got the area covered. Others speculated that the postmen feared getting lost, and so – just in case they suffer sudden and severe memory loss – dropped the rubber bands so that they could follow their trail back to the Post Office.

Realising that the red rubber band project was not achieving what it hoped, in 2012 the Royal Mail switched back to using brown rubber bands once again. Postmen still seem to drop as many of them as before, but now the camouflage makes them less conspicuous to their critics.

For those seeking to save money in any way they can, Royal Mail rubber bands offer a great opportunity. By collecting them up in the street there is no need to buy another rubber band again, and there have been many suggestions for uses for them. These range from the obvious, such as making a catapult, through to a trick for using them to fasten your trousers so that they can automatically expand after a large meal, and, more bizarrely, a technique using rubber bands to make a watermelon explode. ■

M&S underwear

Marks and Spencer, also known affectionately as 'M&S' or 'Marks & Sparks', has been a constant presence on British high streets for 80 years. Though not the force it once was, M&S still sells underwear to around one in four men and one in three women. It also sells many other things: high-quality food advertised on TV with a sultry female voice whispering enticingly: 'This is not just food, this is M&S food', clothing, housewares and most recently banking.

Michael Marks and Tom Spencer started the company in the 1890s. Marks was an immigrant from Poland who set out as a market trader in Leeds, while Spencer was a bookkeeper from Yorkshire. They and their successors went on to build a chain of over 700 shops across the UK, with another 360 more in 40 other countries worldwide.

What made them such an established part of British culture was the retailer's reputation for selling clothes of dependable quality at reasonable prices, as well as their policy of selling only UK-made clothing and accepting returned goods without any challenge. Sadly in recent years M&S has been rather less successful than it once was. In 1998 it became the first UK company to make £1 billion profit in a

single year, but by 2001 this had plunged to £145 million.

The challenge from new trendier rivals has also cut into profits and forced a change of style on M&S, as it has struggled to appeal to younger buyers. In 2010 it launched a range of low-rise underwear, known as the R-Pant, apparently inspired by the Twilight actor Robert Pattinson.

But even some older customers have challenged it in recent years. In 2008 the TV presenter Jeremy Paxman complained that M&S socks wore out faster and did not stay up as well as they once had. But it was the underwear that drew his sharpest criticism. In an email to the M&S Chief Executive he wrote that M&S pants 'no longer provide adequate support. When I've discussed this with friends... it has revealed widespread gusset anxiety. I do feel that someone should take up this mighty battle.'

Whilst this criticism from a well-known television presenter no doubt hurt, you can see it as a measure of the affection that M&S still holds in many people's hearts. Why else would Paxman bother to write to the company when he could have just bought his underwear from somewhere else? ■

Widespread gusset anxiety

Stile

A stile is a simple structure, usually made of wood, that you will find on footpaths all over Britain. It provides access through fences or hedges for walkers, but keeps animals in their place and, unlike a gate, cannot be left open.

Stiles take many forms, but usually consist of one or two steps over a fence, as shown here, or a V shape that the walker has to squeeze through.

In the past stiles were installed on footpaths provided for farmworkers and others to walk from village to village, but today they are mostly used for leisure walking, the result of more than 100 years of campaigning to allow public access to the countryside. It all began as long ago as 1884 when James Bryce MP introduced a bill calling for freedom to roam the countryside. By that time the railways had made it possible for people working in the cities to get out into the country at weekends, but the bill met strong resistance from private landowners and it failed to make it into law.

In 1932 a mass protest by ramblers at Kinder Scout in the Peak District of England led to six people being jailed. Finally in 1949 the National Parks were created and subsequent legislation – most recently the Countryside and Rights of Way (CROW) Act in 2000 – opened up access for people to roam the British countryside. ■

Freedom to roam

Car number plate

The current record paid for a UK car registration is £440,000

British car number plates have to be white at the front of the car and yellow at the back, and use black letters (using a font known as Charles Wright 2001, if you are a student of typefaces). Why they are white at one end and yellow at the other we do not know. Maybe it helps you tell which way the car is pointing?

And if you are a little bit nerdy then you will want to know that the numbering system uses two letters, followed by two numbers and then three letters. The first letter tells you where the car was first registered, so for example you C tells you it is from Cymru (Wales), S from Scotland, L from London, M from Manchester and so on. The two numbers in the middle tell you when the car was first registered.

If you do not mind paying a bit more money you make your car stand out by ordering a personalised plate. Personal number plates offer up whole new possibilities. To boost national income without raising taxes the government sells off some 'interesting' number plates by auction. These are popular with people wanting to make their car stand out from the crowd. Specially favoured are those that make up the driver's name. A Mr Singh paid over £100,000 to buy MR51NGH in 2006, no doubt keen to keep up with his brother who had already bought S1NGH for £86,000 some years earlier. But there are some limits: plates that would make what the licensing authorities consider to be rude words are not allowed.

The current record paid for a UK car registration is almost half a million pounds paid by a British businessman Afzal Khan in 2008 for the registration F1. This was almost twice the value of his car, a Mercedes McLaren, but it is still peanuts compared to the £7.5million paid in Abu Dhabi for the registration 1 in the same year. ∎

Acknowledgements

Thanks to all the people who suggested objects that they felt should be included in this book, especially the British expats who listed the things they missed most from home and the many immigrants, temporary and permanent, who pointed out the oddities that had baffled, amused or interested them most when they moved to live in Britain.

Thanks too to CJ and Helen from the DesignLAB at Manchester School of Art for their encouragement in developing this project.

We are also grateful to the organisations listed below for their help in the production of this book:

Food and Drink
Bitter & Twisted beer: Harviestoun Brewery. Brown Sauce: Wilkin & Sons Ltd. Cadbury's Creme Egg: Kraft Foods. English Mustard: Unilever UK Ltd. Golden Syrup: Tate & Lyle Sugars. Irn-Bru: AG Barr plc. Kendal Mint Cake: George Romney Ltd. Marmite: Unilever UK Ltd. Orange marmalade: Wilkin & Sons Ltd. Polo mint: The 'Polo' name and image is reproduced with the kind permission of Societe des Produits Nestle S.A. Scotch Whisky: Image of Old Pulteney 21 year old courtesy of Inver House Distillers Ltd and Burt Greener Communications. Stinking Bishop cheese: Charles Martell & Son Ltd. Worcestershire sauce: The Lea & Perrins Worcestershire Sauce name and image is reproduced with the kind permission of HJ Heinz Ltd. Laverbread supplied by The Fish Society. Pork Pie: Pork Pie Appreciation Society (www.porkpieclub.com).

Clothing
Barbour jacket: Beaufort jacket courtesy of J Barbour & Sons Ltd. Doc Martens boot: Airwair International Ltd. Fulton umbrella: A. Fulton Co. Ltd. Hunting pink: Image of Grafton Hunt coat courtesy of Mears Country Jackets Ltd. Manchester United football shirt: Manchester United Ltd. Policeman's helmet: Greater Manchester Police. Royal Ascot Ladies' Day Hat: Ilda Di Vico Couture Millinery (www.ascothats.net). School uniform: Photo credit Stockport Grammar School, with thanks for permission to Mr and Mrs Bassi and Rohan Bassi. Folk the Banks T-shirt: Jamie Reid courtesy of Isis Gallery, UK. Wellington boot: Hunter Boot Ltd.

At Home
AGA cooker: AGA Rangemaster Ltd. Anglepoise light: Anglepoise Ltd. Dyson vacuum cleaner: Dyson. Hot-water bottle: quote from George Mikes taken from *How to be a Brit*, Andre Deutsch 1984. Permission courtesy of Penguin Books. Knife, fork and spoon: London cutlery by David Mellor Design Ltd. Teapot: (novelty) The Tea Pottery (www.teapottery.co.uk); (dotty) Emma Bridgwater. Royal Worcester wedding mug: Royal Worcester. Tesco carrier bag: Tesco plc.

Transport and Travel
A-Z street map: Geographers' A-Z Map Co. Ltd. Brompton bike: Brompton Bicycle Ltd. Eddie Stobart lorry: Eddie Stobart Ltd. Hackney carriage: copyright LTI Limited reproduced with permission. Fairway and TX shape is a registered design. FairwayTM, TXTM, the LTI device, the LTI, London Taxis International and The London Taxi Company logos are all trademarks of LTI Limited. JCB 3CX: JC Bamford Excavators Ltd. London Underground map: Transport for London. Mini: photo author: DeFacto. File licensed under the Creative Commons Attribution-Share Alike 2.5 Generic licence.
MINI: BMW UK Ltd. Morgan Three Wheeler: Morgan Motor Co. Ordnance survey map: Ordnance Survey Ltd. Oyster card: Transport for London. Range Rover: Jaguar Land Rover Ltd. Red double decker bus: Transport for London. Rolls-Royce Phantom: Rolls-Royce Motor Cars Ltd.

Sport and Leisure
Red Nose: thanks to Comic Relief. Glamping tent: thanks to Tobyn Cleeves of Bell Tents (www.campingwithsoul.co.uk). Morris dancers' bells and hat: thanks to Duncan Broomhead and Adlington Morris Men. Pantomime Dame's costume: Dame played by Sam Oakes in Cheshire Youth Pantomime Society performance of *Snow White & the Seven Dwarfs*. Photo by Helen Robinson, costume by Sonia Robinson, make-up by Kendal Tyne Love.

Out and About
Argos catalogue: Home Retail Group. Comic seaside postcard: images copyright of Bamforth & Co Ltd. Hille chair: Hille Educational Products Ltd. Mr Whippy ice cream van: Ian Super Whippy Ltd (www.MrWhippy.co.uk). Pub sign: Joseph Holt Ltd. Remembrance poppy: Royal British Legion.

The Authors

Geoff Hall is British. He is a graduate in Modern Languages from Oxford University, and holds a first class degree in Three Dimensional Design and a Masters degree in Design from the Manchester School of Art. In addition to writing on design-related matters he teaches part-time on the Design course at Manchester.

Kamila Kasperowicz came to live in Britain from her native Poland three years ago and is ideally placed to recognise the peculiarities of British people and their everyday culture.
She is a graphic designer, with a first class degree from the University of Silesia. She has recently completed a Masters degree in Design at the Manchester School of Art.

THE BRITISH ISLES

A Trivia Gazetteer

Paul Anthony Jones

£12.99

ISBN: 978-1-84953-322-5

Hardback

Did you know

… that the oldest tree in Wales is a yew in Llangernyw in Conwy, thought to be around 4,000 years old?

… that London is one of only three cities worldwide to have hosted both the Olympic and Commonwealth Games?

… that Ebenezer Place in Wick, Caithness, is officially recognised as the shortest street in the world, at a mere 206 cm (81 in.) in length?

From a Scottish waterfall three times the height of Niagara Falls to the last foreign invasion of Britain and the birthplace of the first Oscar-winning Welshman, *The British Isles: A Trivia Gazetteer* brings together hundreds of remarkable facts and feats each pertaining to a different location in Britain and Ireland. As much an accessible and informative reference book as it is an entertaining miscellany, it aims to expand our knowledge of these extraordinary islands while uncovering and celebrating some of their most remarkable people and places.

BRILLIANT BRITAIN

A Celebration of its Unique Traditions and Customs

Jane Peyton

£9.99

ISBN: 978-1-84953-309-6

Hardback

Brilliant Britain is an entertaining journey through the quirks, oddities and idiosyncrasies that define our nation and preserve us from the mundane and predictable, such as:

- the royal pomp and pageantry of the State Opening of Parliament and the less well-known swan-upping;
- unusual sports and pastimes, from bog snorkelling to worm charming;
- annual countrywide events including the May Day festivities and the beating of the bounds;
- dialects and slang, provincial foods and a recipe for the perfect chip butty.

This book lifts the lid on a rich heritage of eccentricity and diversity, exploring all that makes Britain brilliant.

'British, eccentric and very proud of it. One author's view of the traditions that make us what we are... [Britain's] citizens remain as eccentric as ever and its oldest customs are alive and well'
DAILY TELEGRAPH

If you're interested in finding out more about our gift books, follow us on Twitter: **@Summersdale**

www.summersdale.com